For Steve

"To see a world in a grain of sand
And a heaven in a wild flower,
Hold infinity in the palm of your hand
And eternity in an hour."

–*William Blake*
"Auguries of Innocence"

ACKNOWLEDGMENTS

The author gratefully acknowledges the following sources of art and graphics reproduced in this book and thanks all those who through their critical evaluation have contributed to its completion.

Cover: Original graphic by Steven W. Luther, Santa Fe, New Mexico.

Fig. (1)   Redrawn from Nick Herbert, *Quantum Reality: Beyond the New Physics*, and from Jim Baggott, *The Meaning of Quantum Theory*.

Fig. (2)   Adapted from D. Bohm and B.J. Hiley, *The Undivided Universe*, and from F. David Peat, *Einstein's Moon*.

Fig. (3)   Adapted from D. Bohm and B.J. Hiley, *The Undivided Universe*, and from F. David Peat, *Einstein's Moon*.

Fig. (4)   Following an illustration by Nick Herbert, *Quantum Reality: Beyond the New Physics*.

CONTENTS

PROLOGUE

A few years ago, haunted by the vision that modern science ought to be able to shed some useful light on the meaning of life, I undertook to survey some of the major scientific disciplines from physics to biology, hoping thereby to lift, if ever so slightly, the veil of agnosticism that has been my philosophical lot in life. Never having derived much comfort from religion, I rather naively expected modern science to fill the void by enabling me to construct a sort of natural theology to live by. The results of this exercise were reported in *The Compasses of God*, but they raised as many new questions as they answered.[1] What I found was that modern science, for all its vaunted excellence, has no monopoly on truth and that scientists—for the most part—are simply not interested in pursuing metaphysical questions *as scientists*. Most of them consider such questions to lie outside the domain of science because they involve major discontinuities with which they feel uncomfortable and to which they cannot apply their cherished reductionist methods of analysis. These methods served science well so long as the world was regarded as a giant mechanism, but they do not work nearly so well in today's relativistic and quantum universe. Today's cosmos is seen, not as static and eternal, but as ever-changing and expanding, possibly without limit, amid relentless flux and turbulence. Its invisible counterpart, the microcosmos, is conjectured to be equally turbulent and quixotic—a sea of immeasurable and unpredictable quantum energy. These two worlds, the very large and the very small, are obviously connected, but it has been difficult up to now to unify them in theory because the one—the macro world—is seen as continuous, deterministic, and local while the other—the quantum world—is viewed as discontinuous, probabilistic, and non-local. Beyond this, it seems highly unlikely that a single, final 'theory of everything' is even mathematically calculable in light of the fact that Gödel's incompleteness theorem shows such an objective to be unattainable. Gödel's theorem proves that no mathematical formalism, however encompassing, can contain within itself the confirmation of its own validity. According to Gödel there will always be some truths that lie outside the system so that, in order to provide confirmation of these, a larger and more inclusive algorithm would be required in an infinite regress that could never be final or complete.

These considerations notwithstanding, a number of contemporary physicists are suggesting that a 'theory of everything' may be in sight. Their arrogance, it seems to me, is monumental if we recall the fact that, at the end of the last century, Lord Kelvin—one of the most eminent physicists of his day—was advising young people to avoid the study of physics because almost everything worth knowing had been discovered. Lord Kelvin's colossal misjudgment antedated the relativity and quantum revolutions by only a few years. Today, in the wake of Bell's theorem establishing the fact that local reality theories cannot account for the extraordinary particle correlations predicted by quantum mechanics—a finding that Henry Stapp has called perhaps the most important discovery of physics—a door has been opened on a whole new world of phenomena which Einstein dismissed as "spooky actions at a distance." At the dawn of the twenty-first century the startling new fact of non-locality, now confirmed beyond a reasonable doubt by the Alain Aspect experiments, beckons physicists to expand their mental horizons as the mystery of what constitutes physical reality has once again retreated beyond their grasp. At the dawn of the new century it appears increasingly unlikely that scientists, for all their cleverness, will ever succeed in catching the Almighty in a bottle.

The emerging realization among scientists that the universe is probably a seamless interconnected whole in which superluminal effects in the here and now may owe their origin to remote and perhaps ancient causes has to rank, if correct, as one of the most astounding of modern physics. Newton would have denounced it as absurd and Einstein is known to have rejected it out of hand. It is an idea that is impossible to reconcile with the classical scientific view that the universe is essentially nothing more than a giant mechanism whose interacting parts produce locally predictable effects by pushing or pulling this way and that in response to purely local forces. The metaphysical implications of non-locality are mind-boggling because they are suggestive of a teleology which transcends, yet forms, informs, directs, and influences literally everything that exists. Hardnosed practitioners of science have to ask themselves, if the world is really as odd as all that, whether the time has not come to show metaphysics some respect. Perhaps, indeed, it is time for scientists to invite God back into the universe. It is my belief that recent scientific revelations now make a metaphysical approach to scientific truth far more credible than in the past because there can no longer be any doubt that traditional reductionism has failed. The irreducible fact is that the existence of life, consciousness, intelligence, creativity, beauty, purpose, and order can no longer be ignored in the construction of scientific theories about how the world works. It is my intent in this book to explore the broad outlines of an ontology which recognizes a fundamental reality beyond physics by surveying the contributions of a number of respected thinkers and then extracting from their thoughts such conclusions and speculations as may be congenial to my own.

In *The Compasses of God* I wrote that, far from being on the verge of solving the riddle of the universe, "Man has taken only the very first steps toward knowledge of self and cosmos on what is likely to turn out to be an infinite voyage." Man may never see that voyage to completion, but by his nature he is compelled to undertake it. Whatever man's final destiny may be, he cannot avoid seeking the holy grail of truth, no matter where it may lead him. This notion has been rather well captured in the lyric to *The Quest* from the musical play *Man of La Mancha*.

"...and the world will be better for this,
that one man, scorned and covered with scars,
still strove, with his last ounce of courage,
to reach the unreachable stars."

Martin E.W. Luther,
Minneapolis, Minnesota
October 6, 1995

PART I

PHYSICS

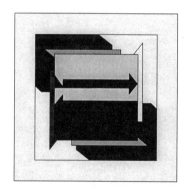

ONE

PERCEIVING REALITY

"I accept the universe."
–Margaret Fuller

"By God, she'd better!"
–Thomas Carlyle

Most of us engaged in the mundane pursuit of making a living naturally assume that the world is real—sometimes all *too* real—on awakening each morning. Getting up is like a dash of cold water in the face. The reality we are compelled to deal with, in competition with our fellow men, is seen as something external to ourselves, something that thrusts itself upon us, whether we like it or not; it *cannot* be ignored. We did not ask to be born into this world but neither do we wish to leave it. The world is simply a 'given' that we have to conquer in order to survive.

The world is our 'reality', and we live in it by necessity, seldom pausing to ask what it means. On occasion, however, the more contemplative among us may demand that the world 'explain itself' when we feel that an injustice has been done. On such occasions we feel that, somehow, proper compensation or restitution ought to be made. Man in every culture has always felt that evil should be punished and merit rewarded. We want the world to be 'fair.' Now, I would like to suggest to you that this perception that the world is 'unfair' reveals an astonishing fact about us. That fact is what Kant called the moral imperative, and it is innate only to humans. Our animal brethren do not ask the world to justify itself to them, only man does that. Why do we expect the world to be 'fair', and why are we so disappointed when it is not? Is there something about us that is not of this world, something which other living creatures do not share? And what does a sense of justice have to do with the world's reality in any event?

Would we expect the world to be 'fair' if we really believed, down deep in our hearts, that it was only a vast illusion? We do not demand that a stage play be fair, because we see it for the artifice that it is, but if the world is actually only a farce then can it have any real personal meaning for us? And isn't then our pathetic demand for 'justice' somehow a profound betrayal?

The very fact that humans ponder such questions suggests to me that man *is* a special creation who occupies a place above all others in the animal kingdom. Man demands to know *why*, and he expects to obtain *justice*, whatever his view of the latter may be. Oddly enough, it is these same attributes of man which also give rise to his science, where the notion of justice takes the form of a faith in the *rational* nature of the world. The assumption that the universe is a place where reason and rationality prevail is one that all scientists implicitly make, or there would be no science. But what is reasonable and rational? Ah, there's the rub! What is reasonable to one scientist may not seem reasonable to another, as we see in the case of Einstein's long-running argument with Neils Bohr over quantum theory. Bohr's contention that quantum events are instantly reified (made real) only when observed drew from Einstein the retort that he did not believe that a mouse, simply by observing the universe, could change it! "No reasonable definition of reality," he asserted, "could be expected to permit this."[2] Reasonable or not, it has now been established beyond reasonable (sic!) doubt that Bohr was at least correct about the quantum world's non-local nature, if not necessarily about its 'reality.' But we are getting into deeper waters than I intend to at this point, so let us return to the theme at hand.

4

In the world of our daily experience, a feeling of 'reality' is given to us by our five senses, those of sight, sound, touch, taste, and smell. A person born without these faculties would, presumably, remain forever imprisoned in a silent tomb from which there was no escape. We can only speculate what the consciousness of such a being must be like, or whether there could even exist a sense of self-awareness. The case of Helen Keller is extraordinary in this connection. Deprived of the senses of sight and sound at nineteen months, she became a deaf-mute, yet subsequently learned to read, write, and speak, acquiring an exceptional education and a proficiency in several languages. She also wrote a half-dozen books and traveled widely. Not many of us, even with all our faculties intact, succeed in probing as deeply the world's infinite variety.

It is quite humbling to realize that, notwithstanding the use of all our senses, we are, as a matter of fact, able to discern directly only a tiny fraction of the world's 'reality.' We are all handicapped by the limited range of our vision and our hearing and the less than acute development of our faculties of taste, touch, and smell, which are far more sensitive in some animals. For example, humans 'see' only about one octave of the more than sixty octave spectrum of electromagnetic radiation, a spectrum that extends beyond the visible to include radio waves, infra red, ultra violet, X-rays, and gamma rays. They 'hear' even less of the total range of sound, including the ultrasonic. It is possible to extend human experience of sight and sound via the use of telescopes, microscopes, auditory devices, and other measuring instruments, but the results obtained are often little more than pointer readings on a scale or computer print-outs, not direct cognition of the event itself. Scientific instruments usually do not put us in direct touch with 'reality.' But are our senses any more reliable?

It may surprise you to be told that, not only are our senses incapable of fathoming more than a small portion of so-called 'reality', but that the portion which they do fathom is not the physicist's 'reality.' All of the sensory impressions we receive from the world are initially registered as physical impulses of one kind or another, either electromagnetic, chemical, or pressure-related. These impulses are carried to the brain from eye, ear, nose, tongue, and skin and somehow magically transformed there into our perceptions of the world. Now, here is the essential point. These perceptions, it cannot be stressed too strongly, are *mental constructs only*, whose qualitative content is unique. They tell us absolutely nothing about the physical phenomena themselves. The sensation of color, for example, cannot be accounted for by the physicist's objective description of light waves. There is a fundamental dichotomy here, apparently unbridgeable, between the sensation that the mind perceives and the phenomenon that science describes. In writing about the chief characteristics of sound perception the founder of wave mechanics, Erwin Schrödinger, states: "...neither the physicist's description nor that of the physiologist contains any trace of the sensation of sound... nerve impulses are conducted to a certain portion of the brain, where they are registered as a sequence of sounds. We can follow the pressure changes in the air as they produce vibrations of the eardrum, we can see how its motion is transferred by a chain of tiny bones to another membrane and eventually to parts of the membrane inside the cochlea, composed of fibres of varying length... We may reach an understanding of how such a vibrating fibre sets up an electrical and chemical process of conduction in the nervous fibre with which it is in touch. We may follow this conduction to the cerebral cortex... but nowhere shall we hit on this as 'registering as sound', which simply is not contained in our scientific picture, but is only in the mind of the person whose ear and brain we are speaking of... So we come back to this strange state of affairs. While the direct sensual perception of the phenomenon tells us nothing as to its objective physical nature... yet the theoretical picture we obtain eventually rests entirely on a complicated array of various informations, all obtained by direct sensual perception. It resides upon them, it is pieced together from them, yet it cannot really be said to contain them." Schrödinger concludes with two observations: "(a) ...that all scientific knowledge is based on sense perception, and (b) that none-the-less the scientific views of natural processes formed in this way lack all sensual qualities and therefore *cannot account for the latter.*"[3] (italics mine)

Matter-of-fact though it may be, I regard this as an astonishing finding. Although there are several dozen different functioning parts in the human ear, the perception of sound cannot be located in any of them. Schrödinger recognizes the profound mystery that this entails and comes to terms with it by concluding that there is no way of explaining the mental in terms of the physical. The qualitative nature of what we hear is unique and quite distinct from its physical nature. The phenomenon called hearing delivers a picture, an emotion, a sensation which cannot be understood as the totality of the operations that produce it, a finding that holds for our other sense perceptions as well. The perceived totality is something else, something ontologically distinct, which is greater than the sum of its parts. The mystery here is of a piece with the old mind/body problem, namely, how are mind and body connected? That there is a dependence between them is clear, but that is all which is clear. The nature of the dependence remains a mystery.

Now, traditionally, when scientists try to unravel a mystery, they employ a principle called *reductionism.* They attempt to reduce the problem to its constituent parts in an effort to understand it. This technique is appealing, common sense, and natural, for we all use it every day in dealing with our lives. However, it has its limits. It is analytical and powerful, but it can cause us to lose sight of the forest on account of all the trees. What the principle fails to recognize is that the whole is not simply the sum of all the parts but is, in fact, *another* reality which is ontologically distinct. This other reality is not simply one that *emerges,* almost automatically, from the collection of the parts but is one that literally requires the presence of consciousness to give it identity and meaning. This is something that science has yet to accept because science cannot account for the reality of mind. Neuroscientists, especially, (with some notable exceptions) are mired in the belief that mind and brain are *identical* and that both can be understood in terms of an analysis of the brain's structure and electrochemical circuitry. Therefore, they insist on examining that circuitry and structure, including the millions upon millions of the brain's neurons and synapses, in the minutest detail, hoping somehow to locate mind or consciousness in the brain's functioning. But they cannot find mind in the brain any more than physicists can find our perceptions in the motions of the atoms that impinge on our senses. They cannot find mind in the brain because mind is not an emergent *physical* property of the brain but a *mental* reality that is ontologically distinct.

This conclusion is to me so obvious that I am surprised that scientists have clung so long to the reductionist fallacy where mind and brain are concerned.[4] To illustrate, take the example of a clock, which lends itself rather well to a description of the reductionist approach. It should be apparent that when we have dismantled a clock and laid out on a bench all of its various springs, screws, belts, weights, and gears, we have not, in so doing, enhanced our understanding of a clock's ontological reality by a single iota. The internal mechanism of a clock is a pile of junk until assembled into a working arrangement. Even then it may be viewed as only a particular arrangement of its parts—possibly one out of many—until the presence of consciousness gives it meaning. A brain, similarly, is a particular arrangement of *its* working parts which can also be laid out on a table and inspected, like the components of a computer. Re-assembled, it may look in every respect like the original, but *there is no consciousness present*. The ontological reality of mind is absent.

The fundamental error of reductionism is to mistake the totality of the parts for the whole. While the principle of reductionism can prove useful in understanding a machine's or an organism's functioning, it can give no hint of the reality of the wholeness associated with that functioning because the wholeness is ontologically separate and distinct. That wholeness is given only by an observing mind.

In the second half of the twentieth century it has become increasingly apparent to many that the world is *holistically* inter-related and that simple reductionism is no longer sufficient as an approach to resolving a number of mankind's philosophical/scientific problems. Just as quantum theory supplanted the old classicism earlier in the century, so a new view incorporating the recently established fact of non-locality is now challenging the unsatisfactory interpretive elements of quantum mechanics. This view, called holism, is frankly metaphysical. It is grand and universal in concept and, in my opinion, rich in explanatory power.

As the new century approaches, it is becoming increasingly obvious to a number of physicists that the rich mental and spiritual tapestry of our lives is simply not translatable, qualitatively, into the mathematical algorithms that physics employs to represent 'reality.' The question then poses itself, why should these mathematical concepts of a shadowy and ephemeral quantum world—a world whose existence, at the very least, is problematical—be accorded a more fundamental 'reality status' than our perceptions, which are immediate, unambiguous, and personal? Is it, perhaps, not foolish to seek in the quantum world's evanescent and indefinable nature the ground of our noetic world's complex form and structure? If, as most quantum physicists contend, it is only our observation of a quantum phenomenon that makes it 'real', how is it possible for our observing minds to 'emerge', retrospectively, from what was created only as a *result* of our observation?

There is clearly something cockeyed about this whole business, centered as it is on the notion of an observer-dependent reality. Physicist John Wheeler has even extended the idea of observer-dependency backward in time, so that man's observation of past events, such as those he observes when he peers out at the galaxies through the lens of a telescope, seems to make him a participant in their occurrence. In Wheeler's "participatory universe," man is perversely seen as present at his own creation!

The mystery of how we perceive and of whether what we perceive is 'real' is one that has been argued by virtually every philosopher, from Aristotle to Kant, largely without result. Although there may be no 'final' answer, I hope to persuade you that there are many levels of reality or truth and that the so-called 'hard' reality of the physical world is not at all what it seems. I

9

hope to persuade you that we have every right to reject as inadequate and barren the still dominant scientific philosophy of reductionism and to look at the world in another way, which is called holism. This is a philosophy which examines the Feynman hierarchy of cause and effect and concludes that its base is not mindless matter but an intelligence which transcends the universe. [5] This philosophy rejects the notion that a nuts and bolts approach to the study of the brain will ever reveal the source of conscious awareness or creative thought. The philosophy of holism recognizes that, to the extent that the whole represents something *different* from the sum of the parts, it cannot be ontologically the *same* as the sum of the parts, any more than any creative work, such as a sculpture or a painting, can be ontologically identified with the materials from which it is made. The philosophy of holism takes the view, which is also that of quantum physics, that the significance of the parts is dependent on the unity and character of the whole, rather than the other way around. Physicist Fritjof Capra has written: "Quantum theory forces us to see the universe, not as a collection of physical objects, but rather as a complicated web of relations between the various parts of a unified whole."[6] Another physicist, David Bohm, has carried the idea of an integrated wholeness much further in developing the concept of an "implicate order," in which everything in the universe is "enfolded" into everything else, as in a hologram.[7] Bohm's concept of the universe as an undivided whole rather than as a collection of fragmented and independently existing parts is not new to philosophers, but it has lain deeply submerged in recent centuries. Though frankly metaphysical in nature, it has not prevented Bohm from formulating a mathematically consistent new theory of the quantum that duplicates in all respects the statistical predictions of the orthodox theory. Bohm's new theory incorporates a factor he calls the *Quantum Potential,* which harks back to the old de Broglie pilot-wave ontology of 1927, about which I shall have much more to say later.

Once again, however, I fear that I am getting ahead of my story. In the next few chapters I shall review some of the anomalies of the old classical physics, so that readers may appreciate the paradoxes which led to the flowering of quantum theory in the early decades of the twentieth century. We shall see how the old physics, which was based on the notion of causality and continuity, gave way to quantum theory, which rejected both assumptions, only to return once again in these closing years of the century to the ideas of wholeness and of interconnectedness. It is a very strange loop that I will be describing, one in which paradoxes abound, but one in which some real progress in the science of physics has been made. If further progress is to be made, it seems to me that all of physics will have to undergo a violent shake-up in the twenty-first century. I am not naive enough to believe, however, that whatever emerges from such a shake-up will provide any 'final' answers. As I have indicated, man may never be able to encompass all of physical reality in a single all-inclusive and final theory, and I have more than a sneaking suspicion that that is the way it was 'meant' to be.

TWO

A REVOLUTION IN PHYSICS

"When you have eliminated the impossible, whatever remains—however improbable—must be the truth."
–Sherlock Holmes,
The Sign of Four

O ne should not use the word 'revolution' lightly, but that is the only way to describe the history of physics in the last hundred years. Physicists, as a group, seem to have taken a leaf out of one of Sherlock Holmes' adventures, finding truth in the improbable by eliminating the impossible. Whenever the great detective ran into a fictional blind alley, he solved the mystery by "eliminating the impossible." In the same manner Max Planck, the so-called 'father' of quantum theory, escaped from the blind alley of the ultraviolet catastrophe—a classical conundrum which no one had been able to solve—by postulating an outrageous alternative, the alternative of discreteness in radiant energy emission. What Planck did was to assume that radiation within the atom was emitted in 'lumps', or quanta, rather than continuously, a most improbable assumption under the rules of classicism. The alternative, however, was impossible, so Planck really had no choice. A solution, he has written, had to be found at "any cost", and Planck found it in the 'improbable' existence of the quantum.

Planck's discovery ultimately led to the development of a

whole new theory of atomic structure and behavior, but Planck had little part in that beyond his initial discovery. In fact, he kept trying to stuff the genie back into the bottle by continuing to seek a more 'classical' solution.

The new quantum theory which Planck had reluctantly fathered was perhaps as improbable as the classical dilemmas that gave rise to it, but it was not "impossible". Bizarre though it was the new theory yielded statistical predictions of the behavior of sub-atomic particles that the old classicism had found it difficult to achieve. It has, in fact, proved so universally useful that it has been described as the most successful scientific theory ever. The new paradigm, however, has had nothing like the ontological certainty of revealed truth. Though a thing of mathematical elegance, quantum theory has remained mired to this day in a kind of mystical and shadowy unreality that make the basic tenets of the old classicism seem like models of precision and clarity.

Though many scientists might be loath to admit it, physics in the twentieth century has taken on a tinge of the mystical. We hear of "black holes" in space, "wormholes", "time warps", "ghost fields", "parallel universes", and "observer-dependent" reality. The world of classical and pre-classical physics, which lasted almost two thousand years, seems to have vanished like the scaffolding on some ancient structure, and a new structure—the quantum universe—has emerged to take its place. This quantum universe is not mechanical and predictable, like the old, but shadowy and perverse. Nothing in it seems to have any substance or reality.

To some extent science has always been speculative, but never more so than since it began seriously to concern itself with the world of sub-atomic phenomena, whose existence has only recently been made manifest. The idea that matter is made up of indivisible and indestructible little units called atoms has been around since the early Greeks, but only within the last two hundred years has the modern atomic concept been developed, and only within the last hundred years have the remaining skeptics been won over. In this Einstein's investigations into the nature of Brownian motion played a major role, during the seminal year of 1905, because it established the reality of the existence of atoms beyond a reasonable doubt. Nonetheless, the world of classical physics was so complacent a community just a century ago that it prompted one of its most distinguished members to declare that "only a few decimal places" needed to be filled in by scientists to complete the temple of their achievement.[8]

That 'temple' was blown sky-high early in the twentieth century by the relativity and the quantum revolutions. To appreciate the importance of these revolutions one has to have some idea of the mind-set which for so long dominated classical physics. The classical mind-set was a natural product of the common sense view of the physical world as one in which forces with calculable effects acted directly upon objects in their vicinity acccording to immutable and eternal laws. It was a world in which causality reigned, and in which there was no appeal from its judgment. The picture was that of a giant mechanism that had been set in motion by some primal force at the Creation, a mechanism that could be counted on to operate with clocklike precision until the "last syllable of recorded time". This huge mechanism was deemed to function quite independently of man and his tinkering. The human race, and life in general, was simply an "accident of time", in Herman Hesse's curious phrase, almost an intruder on the scene. While the concept of atoms formed a part of this classical picture, the microcosmos within the atom was as yet unimagined and unimaginable.

The first break in this classical mind-set came with Planck's invention of the quantum, which was followed in short order by Einstein's paper on special relativity in 1905. With special relativity Einstein introduced the proposition that gravity was not an attractive force between two objects, as Newton had maintained, but that it was a geometric property of space which the presence of matter imposes. Space, said Einstein, had curvature where matter was present, so that the planets had no more freedom to wander from their orbits than a stylus from the grooves of a phonograph disc. Special relativity also postulated that the speed of light, in a vacuum, was constant and independent of the motion of its source. This was a radical departure from the classical notion that speeds of motion were additive, as they appeared to be in the world of experience. Thus, it had seemed obvious that if a person were walking forward in a moving train, his walking speed must be added to the speed of locomotion of the train in order to ascertain his true velocity relative to the ground. Not so, declared Einstein, with respect to the speed of light! The speed of light (in a vacuum) is unique in that it is always the same regardless of its source. The speed of light is constant at around 300,000 kilometers/second whether that light is being emitted from an accelerating object or from an object at rest. The constancy of the speed of light gives rise to such 'crazy' ideas as the twins paradox—the idea that twins can actually grow older at different rates depending on how fast they are moving! Despite the provocative and unfamiliar nature of these ideas, Einstein's relativity remained fundamentally classical in the sense that it harked back to traditional concepts of local forces acting causally in an objectively existing universe.

Quantum physics, on the other hand, turned out to be a horse of another color. It represented a total 180 degree break with classicism. As such, it became the new 'religion' of twentieth century science. Its central challenge to die-hard classicists is: *How can the world be real if the stuff that it is made of is not?* This is a question to which there are no easy answers, and it is one that has thrust metaphysical speculations concerning the nature of reality to center stage in the ongoing quest for scientific 'truth'. Quantum theory has forced us, as Fritjof Capra writes, to view the world, not as an aggregate of independently existing parts, but as a single unified whole. At the level of our daily experience, our macro world, separateness reigns. Discreteness is also present at the level of the quantum. However, the quantum world cannot be understood as simply the sum of its parts. There is a greater reality above and beyond the parts, and the question is whether the parts determine this greater reality or the greater reality the parts. At the most elemental level of matter, at the level of the quantum, the universe appears to end in uncertainty, but it does not end in nothingness. Even the vacuum has structure, and David Bohm has speculated that there may be an infinity of structure beyond this. Structure may, indeed, be "infinite in all directions", in the evocative phrase of Freeman Dyson. The idea has enormous speculative appeal.

Today's physics has come a long way from crude beginnings, but it still contains paradox enough to make you question both the ontological certainty of the classical world and the metaphysical uncertainty of the quantum. The strange irony of this tale is that, by some long and curious loop, the continuity and determinism which characterized the mechanical universe of an earlier era is, paradoxically, re-emerging as one of the most salient—and unexpected—features of the new quantum world.

THREE

WORLDS WITHIN WORLDS

"In solving a problem of this sort, the grand
thing is to be able to reason backward."
–*Sherlock Holmes,*
A Study in Scarlet

The word 'atom' comes from the Greek *atomos* meaning, literally, *uncuttable.* The ancients did not believe that matter could be continually sub-divided but that some limit must eventually be reached, some basic, hard, impenetrable core that would stand revealed as the 'fundamental building block' of nature. The absolute irreducibility of this unit was one of the assumptions on which classical physics was erected.

But atoms are so small that, until Einstein made their existence plausible, most scientists did not really believe in them, while those that did hadn't the shadow of an idea of what they might be like 'inside'. To give some idea of how small they are, consider that a typical atom is only 10^{-8} centimeters across and that its nucleus is 100,000 times smaller. The atom itself is *mostly empty space!* Virtually the entire mass of the atom resides in the nucleus, which may be compared to the size of a grain of salt in the middle of St. Peter's dome. Near the perimeter of the dome are buzzing the electrons, each about the size of a speck of dust! Yet these 'empty' atoms are the basic stuff of the solidity and reality of our material world.

The electrons are envisioned as 'buzzing' around the perimeter of the atom at enormous speed—about 600 miles per second—but no one has ever really 'seen' an electron; we do not really know what they are doing, whether they are point-particles or something else, nor do we know whether they are in fact 'orbiting'. These are just so many 'pictures' that have been drawn up by physicists in order to help them visualize atomic behavior. Ironically, such visualization has no place in orthodox quantum theory. With all the ink that has been spilled by physicists over the quantum 'jump', no one has ever actually witnessed one nor is a 'jump' even actually permitted under orthodox theory. This is another euphemism for the fact that electrons simply mysteriously 'appear' at different locations inside the atom; they are never actually detected *between* 'orbits'—if, indeed, they are 'orbiting'. When they 'jump', they simply radiate or absorb energy by instantaneously appearing at another location. The energy that they emit or absorb in this process is not continuous, as classical theory had assumed, but comes in little discrete 'packages' or *quanta*, instead. It is not known, moreover, why the supposed quantum jumps occur, but it is assumed that the tendency of the system to gravitate toward thermodynamic equilibrium is somehow involved. Within the atom the electrons coexist with the nucleus in an arrangement of forces such that there is an optimal balance between the attraction of the nucleus (which carries a positive charge) and the reluctance of the electrons (which carry a negative charge) to be confined.

The conception of the nucleus and what happens within it has changed dramatically in the last hundred years. Within the nucleus—that grain of 'salt' inside St. Peter's dome—are a number of positively charged protons and an equal number of uncharged neutrons. Protons and neutrons are squeezed rather tightly into the nucleus and their reaction to this confinement is extremely violent. They move about in the nucleus at speeds of 40,000 miles per second—a little more than one-fifth the speed of light—which implies that relativistic effects on time and mass are produced. The nucleus is held together by the so-called 'strong' force, one of the four fundamental forces of nature. It is a very short-range force that becomes powerfully attractive when the nucleons [as protons and neutrons are called] approach within a few diameters of one another, but which then reverses and becomes equally repulsive if they try to move even closer. The nuclear force thus keeps the nucleus in an extremely stable, if highly dynamic, equilibrium.

The picture of the atom as a hard and impenetrable building-block of nature has dissolved, under the gaze of modern science, into one that is altogether more nebulous, one in which the atom's core—the nucleus—has now become the center of attention. Not only are the neutrons inside it subject to spontaneous disintegration, a process known as beta decay, but they can be broken up into several hundred more 'elementary' particles when they are forced to collide with others of their kind which have been accelerated to enormous velocities in cyclotrons. These 'elementary' particles, in turn, are thought to consist of even tinier entities, called quarks and gluons, which are another fifteen powers of ten smaller than the nucleus. And beyond that, it is theorized, lies something called "super-strings", each only 10^{-33} centimeters long, a number so small as to be literally incomprehensible.

To date more than two hundred 'elementary' particles have been discovered through collisions in cyclotrons. The strange thing about them, when they collide with other particles in these high-energy accelerators, is that the shattered remains are not smaller than the original particles! The shattered remains are again particles created out of the kinetic energy of the collisions. The sub-atomic particles are thus both destructible and indestructible at the same time! Moreover, they are "not made of any material stuff", affirms Fritjof Capra. "When we observe them, we never see any material substance; what we observe are dynamic patterns continually changing into one another—a continuous dance of energy."[9] In these high-energy experiments matter is created out of pure energy and then vanishes again into energy, all of this in far less than a millionth of a second. Some of the 'lives' of these particles are so short that they have been dubbed 'virtual'; they pop in and out of existence in a time span so short that the quantum uncertainty principle allows even the law of the conservation of energy to be—briefly—violated!

How do we know that these particles really exist? Well, for one thing, they leave evidence of their ghostly presence behind in the faint tracks on photographs taken in so-called "bubble" chambers. The significance of such tracks and whether they are in fact continuous has been a matter of some dispute.[10] The problem is that, in the quantum world, concepts like 'location' and 'material substance' lose their meaning, in any sense but the mathematical. All of the activity which is evidenced in the break-up of an atomic particle appears as an inseparable web of dynamic energy patterns.

In quantum electro-dynamics [Q.E.D.], which is a merger of classical field theory with quantum mechanics, "The quantum field", writes Fritjof Capra, "is seen as the fundamental physical entity... Particles are merely local condensations of the field, concentrations of energy which come and go, thereby losing their individual character and dissolving into the underlying field."[11] It was also Einstein's opinion that "We may therefore regard matter as being constituted by the regions of space in which the field is extremely intense... There is no place in this new kind of physics both for the field and matter, for the field is the only reality."[12]

The field is the only reality! How far a road we have traveled from the early Greeks! And, yet, that is the conclusion toward which modern physics has been moving as we progress from Schrödinger's wave mechanics to Bohm's Quantum Potential. But, if there are no 'building-blocks' in the classical sense, of what, then, is our apparently solid universe made?

The answer may surprise you, because in this new Land of Oz there is not even a wizard behind the curtain. There is simply the mystery of a stark and inexplicable void. Yet this cannot be the 'final' answer, because it leaves no room for faith, either of the religious kind or the kind that has always motivated physicists to seek for truth in what they believe to be a reasonable and a rational world. Ultimately, in both science and religion, there must be a more satisfying explanation, because in the deepest fibre of their being both physicists and ordinary mortals alike believe the world to be sane and rational. Sane and rational perhaps, but not necessarily comprehensible!

FOUR

THE PARADOXES
OF PHYSICS

"The most dangerous thing in the world is
to leap a chasm in two jumps."
–*Lloyd George*

One of the most famous paradoxes of history is that of Zeno, the Greek, who 'proved', mathematically, that motion was impossible! Suppose, said Zeno, we imagine a mythical race between Achilles, swiftest of the gods, and a slow-moving tortoise. Because of Achilles undoubted advantage, let us give the tortoise a head start to 'level the playing field', as the modern expression goes. Even then, said Zeno, I can prove to you that Achilles will never catch up to the tortoise! Here is the reason why: In the time it takes Achilles to reach the spot where the tortoise was a moment ago, the tortoise—slow though it be—will have moved ahead. Then, in the time it takes the swift Achilles to reach the next spot, the tortoise will have advanced again, so that, no matter how often this sequence is repeated, the tortoise will always be slightly ahead. Hence, Achilles can *never* entirely catch up!!

When we first encounter this conundrum, it generally boggles the mind. Obviously there is something wrong, but what?

It may surprise you to learn that the paradox of Achilles and the tortoise [sometimes transmogrified into hare and turtle] has

23

puzzled some of the best minds through the ages. In this arresting tale logic clashes head-on with common sense. The deadly 'hook' in the paradox is the phrase "in the time that", which seems to imply that we can infinitely divide time into shorter and shorter intervals until we have virtually brought it to a stop. Thus, if one is compelled to think of the race in terms of a succession of constantly diminishing discrete intervals of time, the absurd conclusion is unavoidable. If we could stop time, we could, of course, also stop the race. Time, however, cannot be halted by a mathematical trick. This forces us to consider what the nature of time really is, in relation to motion, an exercise which gets us into some deep waters of contemporary physics.

Zeno's paradox of motion is one of the most perplexing in physics because it points up the apparent irreconcilability of the notions of continuity and discreteness that we accept as normal accompaniments to our everyday lives. We seldom question the contradiction, but in science various attempts to organize the universe exclusively in terms of one or the other of these concepts have led to no end of difficulties.

Take, for example, the mathematical concept of a line. A line, as we commonly understand it, is continuous in nature and yet, in a mathematical sense, a line can be viewed as a number of discrete segments each of which can be infinitely sub-divided, approaching zero as a limit. The mathematical concept of a line is the juxtaposition of an infinite series of dimensionless points. But what, pray tell, is a dimensionless point? If we think of a line in this way, it is hard to see how discreteness can ever give way to continuity, because infinity times zero is still zero. The parallel with Zeno's paradox is striking. In Zeno's paradox a vanishing discreteness apparently stops time and motion, although we know, in fact, that this is not so. In the line paradox the same vanishing discreteness apparently makes continuity impossible. How can these paradoxes be resolved? Is the 'real' world discrete or is it continuous? Or is it, perhaps, both? And if it is *both*, how is such a thing possible?

In my opinion, both discreteness and continuity are free constructs of the human mind. These concepts help us to rationalize the world we live in, but they do not possess an independent existence of their own. The universe is simply a given that can be understood *only* in terms of the unity of opposites, a point of view that I call *dualism* and to which Neils Bohr gave the name of *complementarity.* In ancient Chinese thought it is referred to as *yin* and *yang* and is symbolized by an intriguing diagram that is reproduced below. The diagram, called *T'ai-chi T'u,* contains two dots suggesting that every time one of the two opposite forces of *yin* and *yang* approaches an extreme, it already contains within itself the seed of its opposite. Neils Bohr, one of the founders of quantum theory, found the *T'ai-chi T'u* so fascinating that he adopted it as his family's personal coat of arms.

ANCIENT CHINESE
'DIAGRAM OF THE SUPREME ULTIMATE'

THE T'AI-CHI T'U

The yin/yang concept is a profound one that has been much more highly developed in eastern than in western thought. In western thinking the notion of linear continuity, not cyclicality, remains dominant, and troublesome encounters with discreteness, as in Zeno's paradox, are hard to explain. The world of classical physics was not one of discreteness, but of continuity. In the classical view of things this world had been set in motion at the Creation and it was expected to run without hitch 'forever'.

But around the end of the nineteenth century, even as Lord Kelvin was pontificating about the achievements of physics, scientific faith in the perfection of a mechanical universe began to crumble. There was, in particular, the unresolved puzzle of black body radiation [one of Lord Kelvin's "two small clouds"] that classical physics simply could not explain. A black body in physics is any perfectly absorbing sealed hollow container (exhibiting a small perforation) which can be heated to high temperatures. When such a body is heated, the heat energy inside turns into electromagnetic radiation, with the energy of this radiation steadily rising. With continued heating the energy inside the black body was expected to increase in proportion to the square of the frequency of the radiation produced, resulting ultimately in the production of extreme amounts of energy—the so-called "catastrophe in the ultra-violet." However, nothing like this actually occurs. Instead, the statistical curve of the radiant energy emitted by a black body falls off to zero at extreme frequencies after rising to a peak somewhere around the middle range. How can this be, if Maxwell's classical assumption of an energy *continuum* is correct? The black body puzzle was one that had physicists totally stumped.

The answer that was given by a German physicist, Max Planck, who had been studying the mystery for years, shook the world. Planck, an old-school classicist, finally concluded—"in desperation" as he put it—that the radiant energy from a continually heated black body did not become infinite in the ultra-violet because the energy was not, in fact, being emitted *continuously*. Instead, Planck hypothesized, the energy is emitted in tiny 'lumps', a description to which Einstein later gave the name of *quanta*. Its emission is not continuous, but discrete. These quanta, Planck speculated, were of varying sizes depending on the frequency of the radiation emitted. While a quantum of energy might be very large at the extreme end of the frequency scale, corresponding to the intensity of the radiation at these frequencies, only a few of such high-energy quanta were actually present. At the opposite end of the frequency scale, i.e. at low frequencies and low temperatures, the emitted quanta were small but numerous. Most of the energy of a heated body was thus clustered around the middle of the frequency range where both the size and the number of emitted quanta were 'average'.

The relationship between energy and frequency, Planck found, was given by a formula, $E = h\nu$, where h is a new constant derived directly from the known shape of the radiation curve itself. The value of h, which has since become known as Planck's constant, is a number so tiny that it literally cannot be comprehended.[13] Small as it is, though, it plays a central role in the new theory of quantum physics. The fact that h is so small means, practically speaking, that discreteness at the quantum level does not make itself felt in our everyday world. If h were not trivially small, but large enough to affect that world, all sorts of strange things might happen. A pitched baseball, for example, could not be hit by a batter because, in quantum terms, its location as it approached him would be 'fuzzy' and indeterminate! If, on the other hand, h were zero, there would be no need for a theory of quantum physics, for the laws of classical physics would adequately explain everything. If h were, in fact, zero, black body radiant energy could indeed become infinite, with disastrous consequences for all concerned.

I am getting ahead of myself a little bit here, because what I have just told you has to do with something called the Uncertainty Principle, which Werner Heisenberg found to be an inherent feature of quantum discreteness. There are many other bizarre consequences of this same principle that I want to discuss later. For the moment I simply want to emphasize that Planck's speculation that energy comes in 'lumps', and is not *continuous*, was a radical idea for which there was absolutely no basis in classical physics. What Planck had done was to meld an outrageous discontinuity onto the body of classical physics simply because he could find no other explanation, and he was almost laughed out of court (by some) for his efforts. Physicists *hate* discontinuities because of their *ad hoc* nature. Explaining something by means of a discontinuity seems to them like invoking the miraculous, and is therefore to be avoided if at all possible. As Louis de Broglie, inventor of the "pilot wave" concept, later commented: "On the day when quanta, surreptitiously, were introduced, the vast and grandiose edifice of physics found itself shaken to its very foundation."[14] By postulating the emission of energy in discrete units rather than in terms of a continuous energy spectrum, Planck had been able to solve a problem that had been inexplicable in Newtonian terms and which, as Einstein pointed out, would remain forever inexplicable in those terms. But the cost of explaining it in quantum terms was not trivial. As we shall see, Planck's speculation opened up a Pandora's Box of new and perplexing mysteries, which only multiplied in number as other physicists seized on Planck's idea and applied it to everything material and immaterial in the new and kaleidoscopic quantum world.

The discreteness of Planck's constant, h,—the fact that it is not zero—means that we can never probe the quantum world to its limits, because there is an irreducible uncertainty at its foundation. The paradox of quantum uncertainty is essentially the same one with which Zeno flummoxed his contemporaries more than 2000 years ago. How does the 'river' of energy at the macro level appear to flow smoothly and continuously if, at bottom, it is really 'chunky' and discrete? Is it all an illusion, in the same way that a continuous motion picture film consists of a rapid sequence of still images? From a personal perspective a world that ends in this kind of ambiguity and uncertainty is neither emotionally nor intellectually satisfying. The more important question, it seems to me, is whether Planck's monumental discovery—a discovery that led within a few decades to the full flowering of the new theory of quantum mechanics—is indeed the last word on how the universe is put together. There is enough evidence to the contrary to at least justify the question. The greatest physicist of our time, Albert Einstein, remained unconvinced of quantum theory's claim to completeness, and a number of other physicists have shown that alternative theories are possible. I shall be exploring some of these with you later.

FIVE

THE QUANTUM CONNECTION

"We all agree that your theory is crazy. What we are
not sure of is whether it is crazy enough."
—*Neils Bohr*

I have already indicated that some physicists gave Planck's solution of the black body problem the cold shoulder, perhaps because they saw in it what they regarded as a mathematical trick; it was seen by them as a patchwork, a not wholly tenable result. An important exception was Einstein, who recognized the fundamental importance of Planck's innovation and proceeded to apply it to his own investigation of what is known as the *photoelectric effect*.

The photoelectric effect was, like the black body problem, another of those enigmas of physics that seemed to have no explanation under ordinary classical rules. What happens in the photoelectric effect is that, under certain conditions, a beam of high-frequency (ultra-violet) light, when focused on a polished strip of metal, forcibly dislodges electrons from the metal exactly as if the beam had the force and energy of a hail of bullets. How this was possible if light consisted purely of waves, as was almost universally assumed at the time, remained unexplained. Waves are obviously not like hard particles. When they encounter an obstacle, they disperse, move around it, and coalesce again on the other side, in the manner of water waves approaching a barrier. In doing so they give rise to an interference effect as the crests and troughs of the separate waves meet and either reinforce one another or cancel out. The result is that the energy of the reconstituted wave is either enhanced or diminished by the confluence.

When Einstein explained the photoelectric effect [in a 1905 paper for which he received the Nobel Prize] as resulting from *a shower of particles* of light—not waves—he not only adopted Planck's notion of quantized energy but he also partially resuscitated Newton's old corpuscular theory, a theory that had long seemed hopelessly outdated. As John Gribben has commented, "only a genius or a fool" would have dared to do this since Huygens' wave theory of light was about as firmly entrenched at the time as the theory of the luminiferous ether. Einstein, supremely confident in his own powers of reason, quietly dispatched them both. In the photoelectric effect he pragmatically selected from both the wave and the particle theories of light those elements which he thought valid. Toward the end of his career he nevertheless confessed that in fifty years of *Grübelei* (brooding) he had not penetrated any closer toward an understanding of light's true nature.

After 1905 Einstein's major interest drifted in the direction of relativity, the physical theory that fired the public's imagination and made Einstein's virtually a household name. 1905 was a seminal year in which the young Einstein, almost as an afterthought while working as an examiner in the Swiss patent office in Berne, single-handedly laid down the law on Brownian motion, the photoelectric effect, and relativity. If he had never again had a single thought in his head, this alone would have earned him the accolade of history. It fell, however, to another group of brilliant physicists to bring Planck's notion of quantized energy to full fruition in the development of a new quantum theory of atomic structure and behavior. In Denmark, and thereafter in Germany, Austria, and England, the revolution went quietly forward. It reached a pinnacle in the years 1925-27 with the almost simultaneous promulgation of three separate and distinct approaches to quantum theory on the part of a German, an Austrian, and an Englishman. The groundwork for this explosion of scientific brilliance was laid by an unassuming Dane named Neils Henrik David Bohr.

Neils Bohr was a man who—as Einstein once commented—"utters his opinions like one perpetually groping and never like one who believes he is in possession of definite truth."[15] Nevertheless, Bohr, in an overall sense, exerted at least as large an influence on twentieth century physics as did Einstein, the more popular figure. Bohr, the inventor of the 'old' quantum theory, was the *yin* to Einstein's *yang* in their running debate on the meaning and completeness of quantum theory. In the years after 1905, when Einstein was absorbed in relativity, it was mainly Bohr who continued to search for a more viable theory of the atom and its structure than had been available to that time. And it was mainly Bohr who, through his researches, attracted to his Institute in Copenhagen that brilliant coterie of young scientists which eventually 'solved' the problem of the atom's structure. Their solution was, in a manner of speaking, "worse than the disease" because, as we shall see, it was so abstruse that no humanly comprehensible meaning could be attached to it.

The experiments of Thompson and Rutherford some years before had shown that there was a powerful mutual attraction within the atom so that, under classical rules, the atom did not seem to have any right to exist. Under classical rules the atom should have undergone almost instantaneous collapse, since the electrons thought to be 'orbiting' the nucleus would be suffering a constant loss of energy through acceleration. But this did not happen. The electrons did not spiral in toward the nucleus. The atom was inexplicably stable. Once again, Newtonian physics was stumped. Classical physical principles simply could not provide an answer.

Faced, like Planck, with the necessity of finding a solution almost at "any cost", Bohr decided—like Einstein before him—to grasp the nettle of discreteness that Planck had offered him. Bohr decided to simply disregard the classical assumption of a continuous loss of energy on the part of the atom's orbiting electrons by taking over lock, stock, and barrel the Planck idea that the atom does not radiate energy *continuously* but emits it, rather, in discrete little 'lumps'. Bohr, in effect, made an end run around the problem by introducing another outrageous discontinuity into physics, namely, the notion of the *quantum 'jump'*. Bohr theorized that the atom's electrons orbited the nucleus *only at specific energy levels,* and that these energy levels, or "shells", were arranged around the nucleus on the order of a series of descending steps. Bohr surmised that these steps corresponded to the atom's spectral lines, which are the sharp, dark lines that, under a microscope, are seen as separating one frequency from another. In an atom such lines are produced when the atom either emits or absorbs energy with a very precise frequency, that is, when one of its electrons makes a 'quantum jump'.

The notion of the quantum jump appeals to the imagination somewhat in the same way as the later popularization of the concept of black holes. The quantum jump is utterly mysterious. The electron, in effect, emits a little 'pulse' of energy as it 'jumps' from one energy level to another, but what in the world is this 'jumping' like? As John Gribben points out, it is somewhat like Mars suddenly disappearing from its orbit around the sun and re-appearing instantaneously in the orbit of the earth, while radiating away into space a huge 'pulse' of energy. Actually, it is even weirder than that, because we cannot be sure that what re-appears is, in fact, Mars; it might be, in terms of the atomic model, not the same but another electron![16]

It is at this point for the first—but not the last—time that quantum theory begins to take leave of our senses. Progressively, we have moved from the idea that the transmission of energy within the atom is not continuous, like a line, but discrete, like a point, to the notion that the carrier of this energy—the electron— nevertheless 'jumps' from one location to another, instantaneously, *without ever appearing at any location in-between.* We are then told that this 'jumping' can take place in either ascending or descending order within the atom, at any time, for no reason whatever.

The ultimate extension of this notion became what is known as the *Copenhagen Interpretation* of quantum theory, in which it was argued that the electron could not be said to *have* any real existence at all when it was not observed in a particular location. One could not even be sure, admitted Bohr, that there *was* even a quantum world![17] The electrons which jumped about in such a mysterious fashion were not 'real'—they were only a representational fiction!

Jumping Jehoshaphat! No wonder that Einstein rebelled. With one stroke Bohr had not only 'explained' the atom's stability, but he had succeeded in demolishing the principles of causality and continuity on which the entire edifice of classical physics rested. He had also, perhaps without realizing it, introduced a subtle new notion into physics, the notion of non-locality. He had, in effect, sacrificed all of classical physics—indeed, all of physical 'reality'—to explain a single anomaly. This was scientific progress with a vengeance!

Bohr's insights made sense only if one did not try to visualize them too concretely; his model remained a hodgepodge of quantum and classical ideas. Furthermore, he appeared merely to have exchanged one mystery for another, namely, the mystery of quantum 'jumping' [which Schrödinger could not abide] for the mystery of the atom's stability. Many things remained to be explained, among them the splitting of the atom's spectral lines and the enigma of radioactive decay, but not much further progress was achieved until a brilliant young German, Werner Heisenberg, had what might in theological circles be called a *revelation*.[18]

SIX

THE UNCERTAINTY PRINCIPLE

"This principle is so perfectly general that no particular application of it is possible."
–George Polya

Werner Heisenberg is usually called the 'inventor' of the modern quantum mechanics because it was he who, like Moses, first ascended the mountain—the small North Sea island of Helgoland—and brought back the tablets. In truth, however, the invention of quantum mechanics was more like a joint effort in which genius fed on genius among a small group of young scientists challenged by new concepts and ideas. The key to the breakthrough was a notion that Heisenberg had picked up at the University of Göttingen that a physical theory should be concerned with what could actually be observed through experiment—what Heisenberg termed "observables". Heisenberg therefore determined to junk all notions of 'orbits', which could not be observed but only inferred, and to concentrate instead on formulating a mathematical approach to the atom's structure that would account for what was actually known about its behavior, in particular the observability of its spectral lines. The use of the word *revelation* in this regard somehow seems especially appropriate because Heisenberg writes of experiencing a strange ecstasy. It is a fact that the human mind on occasion does have flashes of insight, whether in physics, mathematics, music, art, or literature, that seem to come from out of the blue, perhaps from the depths of the unconscious. Whatever it was that inspired Heisenberg, he returned quite agitatedly from his solitary meditations to face his colleagues with a new atomic theory in hand, or at least the makings of one. The new theory was based on the mathematical concept of matrices, a form of algebra invented a century earlier by William Hamilton. Matrices follow a strange logic where multiplication is concerned. It is said that matrices do not "commute". What this means is that the product of A X B does not always equal the product of B X A. In matrix algebra the correct result of the multiplication of two numbers depends on the *order* in which they are multiplied. In practical terms this means that measurements on a physical system can give different answers depending on which measurement is done first. Matrix algebra is rather like putting on one's shoes and socks; it matters crucially to the outcome which is donned first!

It turned out that Heisenberg's insight was fundamental, so that when alternative quantum theories were developed by both Schrödinger and Dirac, the same principle of noncommutativity applied. Despite major differences of form and substance, all three theories yielded the same theoretical results. Deeply embedded in each is the notion that so-called *conjugate variables,* such as an atom's position and momentum, do not "commute", that is, both cannot be determined with precision simultaneously. Any attempt to do so is like trying to focus the lens of a camera on two different objects at once. In adjusting the first focus, the second necessarily becomes blurred. A clear sighting of both objects together thus is impossible. Heisenberg found the relationship between conjugate variables to be such that the amount of error in fixing the one variable multiplied by the amount of error in fixing the second variable is always proportional to h, the enigmatic constant that Planck had discovered.[19]

The property of non-commutativity is pervasive in quantum

mechanics, and it leads directly to Heisenberg's famed *Uncertainty Principle*. Heisenberg's discovery of this principle represents the final break of quantum theory with the classical realm and is central to understanding what quantum mechanics is all about. Quantum uncertainty not only challenges everything of a classical nature, it also challenged Einstein's intuition of the way things 'ought to be'. His famous dictum, *God does not play dice*, was Einstein's way of rejecting quantum uncertainty and of reaffirming the classical doctrine of causality. For with quantum uncertainty the scientific assumption that effects have causes goes out the window, and we are left with an ontological vacuum concerning the nature of ultimate reality.

The Uncertainty Principle tells us that at the heart of quantum mechanics there is an inherent and irreducible 'fuzziness' when we attempt to fix precisely the nature of physical reality. Certain properties of a quantum entity, the principle avers, are innate, while others are held to be contextual. Those which are contextual are said to exist, not as real properties of the thing observed [properties such as mass, charge, and spin, for example] but as properties that have a meaning only in a *measurement* context. In the latter category, orthodox quantum theorists maintain, are such things as an electron's position and its momentum, as well as such variables as time and energy. Because time and energy are held to be conjugate, it is theoretically possible for an arbitrarily small fluctuation in energy to persist for an arbitrarily long period of time. Some quantum cosmologists have sought in this manner to explain the origin of the universe as a *quantum fluctuation* arising out of the immense latent energy of the vacuum in accordance with Heisenberg's Uncertainty Principle.

Whether or not you believe this—and Einstein certainly did not—indeterminacy is central to the dogma of quantum theory. The Uncertainty Principle insists that, where conjugate variables are concerned, the more precisely we attempt to fix the value of one variable, the more 'blurred' the other one becomes, so that we can never *as a matter of principle* ever obtain absolute precision with respect to the simultaneous measurement of both. The price of precision in the measurement of one variable is a *residual uncertainty*, proportional to h, in the measurement of the other.

Thus Planck's constant, h, minuscule though it may be, turns out to have a huge physical, as well as metaphysical, significance, a significance which harks back to the paradox of Achilles and the tortoise. Zeno claimed that, if one analyzes the race as an infinitely decreasing series of units of time approaching zero as a limit, then no motion can take place. Achilles can never catch the tortoise. The conclusion is erroneous because motion is by definition continuous and as such is independent of time's measurement.

Now, in physics, when we attempt to assign precise values to the position and velocity of a sub-atomic particle, a somewhat similar paradox arises. Quantum physics says that we cannot assign precise values to position and velocity at the same time because infinite precision with respect to the measurement of the one variable can only be obtained at the expense of infinite *im*precision in the measurement of the other. Even in classical physics, where the limit of precision is not h, or where h is effectively zero, the notion of infinite precision in the measurement of a moving particle runs into conceptual difficulties, because the precise position of a moving particle is not a well-defined concept. As Zeno's paradox demonstrates, there is an essential ambiguity between the notion of a particle at absolute rest, that is, having a fixed position, and the concept of continuous motion. There is an inherent contradiction, producing a logical block in our thinking, when we try to reconcile absolute rest (fixity of position) with *continuous* motion, for *continuous* motion implies that there is *never* a time of absolute rest. In classical physics we overcome this ambiguity mathematically by allowing the residual uncertainty in the simultaneous measurement of two conjugate variables to fall to zero, but in quantum physics the residual uncertainty remains proportional to h. We cannot, in theory, increase our precision beyond this in any simultaneous measurement, although we can measure either variable independently as accurately as we please. The uncertainty is inherent in the equations.

The question is, does the uncertainty also correspond to *reali-*

ty, or is it simply a characteristic of quantum theory? On this point there is considerable dispute, not only because quantum mechanics has shown itself to be immensely successful in application but also because of the inherent paradox of time and motion to which Zeno so cleverly alluded. Physicist David Bohm was not at all convinced. Bohm has argued that quantum uncertainty is not necessarily absolute but is possibly only a consequence of the structure of quantum theory. In a reformulation of quantum theory that Bohm undertook in the 'fifties and 'sixties he concluded that:

> "There is good reason to assume the existence of a sub-quantum mechanical level that is more fundamental than that at which the present quantum theory holds. Within this new level could be operating qualitatively new kinds of laws, leading to those of the current quantum theory as approximations and limiting cases in much the same way that the laws of the atomic domain lead to the macroscopic domain. The indeterminacy principle would then apply only at the quantum level and would have no relevance at lower levels. The treatment of the indeterminacy principle as absolute and final can then be criticized as constituting an arbitrary restriction on scientific theories, since it does not follow from the quantum theory as such, but rather from the assumption of the unlimited validity of certain of its features..."[20]

I do not want to get into the details of Bohm's reformulation of quantum theory here; readers will find the matter dealt with in Chapter 13. I merely want to point out that the concept of uncertainty as Heisenberg developed it is a problem of *measurement* as well as one of the definition of certain "observables". We know very well, in fact, that continuous motion *is* a reality, even though orthodox quantum theory claims to have no knowledge of it.

Orthodox quantum theory disdains even the reality of a quantum world. It was precisely this 'know-nothing' attitude of orthodox quantum theorists that caused Einstein and Schrödinger so much grief and ultimately led to David Bohm's defection as well.

It deserves mentioning that the Uncertainty Principle was actually given a different interpretation when it was first discovered by Heisenberg, one in which the physical 'disturbance' of the quantum entity being observed is held to be the source of the imprecision in its measurement rather than the inherent limitations of the theory itself. Heisenberg himself did not immediately recognize the double twist. His initial attempt to explain uncertainty involved a *Gedankenexperiment* featuring a microscope in which a high-frequency beam of gamma rays is being focused on a moving electron in order to precisely fix its position. Heisenberg realized that this would create a problem, because the energy of such a high-powered beam would knock the electron off course in an unpredictable way, thus making any precise determination of its momentum impossible. If the energy of the probing beam were lowered by reducing its frequency, then its wave length would be too long to accurately fix the electron's position. It seemed that one could not have it both ways. Either the electron's velocity would be uncontrollably accelerated or its position would become 'fuzzy' owing to the disturbance of the viewing instrument. Hence the physical disturbance of the observed object resulting from the intrusion of the viewing instrument made precise measurement impossible. It was Heisenberg's initial opinion that this was what lay at the root of the Uncertainty Principle.

Neils Bohr rather quickly disabused Heisenberg of this "disturbance" interpretation. Bohr argued that the microscope experiment needlessly assumed that the electron actually *possessed* the properties of position and momentum prior to measurement, an assumption derived from classical analogies and not directly verifiable in fact. The assumption, moreover, was one that was obviated by Heisenberg's own theory, the mathematics of which contained all the formalism that was really required. Why go beyond this formalism, Bohr argued? There was no need to look for any physical counterpart in terms of "disturbance" to explain what was already inherent in the theory.

With this argument of Bohr's whatever assurance there was that the new quantum science was bringing us closer to a true understanding of nature than classical physics had been capable of dissolved into meaninglessness. Bohr saw no need to really believe in a quantum world. It was Bohr's position, as noted earlier, that the quantum world is not 'real', but only an abstraction from the mathematics, a point of view that became the basis for the so-called *Copenhagen Interpretation* of quantum theory and which irritated Einstein, in particular, no end.

It was one thing to say that the world could not be measured precisely and quite another to say that, until measured, it didn't really exist. As Stanley L. Jaki, a Hungarian physicist who is also an ordained priest, has pointed out, there is a difference between operational and ontological exactness. Jaki writes: "Had Heisenberg sensed something about the inherent limitations of the methods of physics, he would have refrained from stating that the inability of physicists to measure nature exactly showed the inability of nature to act exactly."[21] But Heisenberg had become a convert. In his *Physics and Philosophy*, published 1958, Heisenberg states: "The ontology of materialism rested upon the illusion...that the direct 'actuality' of the world around us can be extrapolated into the atomic range. This extrapolation...is impossible...atoms are not things...are not real...they form a world of potentialities and possibilities rather than one of things or facts."[22]

These few quotes, to which others might be added, give the flavor of the thinking of the early *Copenhagenists*. They show how far the metaphysics behind quantum theory was removed from traditional classical concepts of reality already in the early decades of this century. It was the Copenhagenists' outright rejection of the existence of an independent reality apart from their measurements that most frustrated Einstein, who argued with them through the rest of his life. "Do you really believe the moon exists only when you are looking at it?" was the question Einstein addressed to his friend and biographer, Abraham Pais. The paradox here is that the moon, like all macroscopic objects, is composed of quantum entities, about each of which there is an inherent uncertainty. At what point, Einstein was asking, does this inherent uncertainty at the quantum level become translated into objective certainty at our level of experience? Or, to phrase the question as I did earlier, "How can the world be real if the stuff that it is made of is not?" This is a paradox that is not resolved by the fact that the quantum of action, h, is microscopically small. Theoretically, the uncertainty relations allow the whole universe to be created out of nothing provided it vanishes once again before the law of conservation of energy, the First Law of Thermodynamics, is violated. In quantum theory this is not at all impossible. Physicists will tell you that 'virtual' particles are being created out of the vacuum "all the time". Physicist Fritjof Capra, author of *The Tao of Physics*, has written: "The vacuum is far from empty. On the contrary, it contains an unlimited number of particles which come into being and vanish without end... The vacuum is truly a 'living void', pulsating in endless rhythms of creation and destruction. The discovery of the dynamic quality of the vacuum is seen by many scientists as one of the most important findings of modern physics."[23]

Is it conceivable that the whole universe could, at bottom, be nothing more than a vacuum fluctuation resting on the questionable reality of a sea of 'virtual' particles constantly popping up out of nothing? Is it conceivable that the moon might not really be 'out there' and could vanish at any time, like Alice's cheshire cat, leaving only a grin? Try telling that to the twelve American astronauts who left their footprints, and their flag, on its soil...

With speculations of this kind we are getting into deep waters. However, I do not want to leave the subject of quantum uncertainty without mentioning its implications for classical causality. The uncertainty relations in quantum mechanics do not directly break with causality, but they do break with determinacy. There is a fine distinction. A quantum event, such as the quantum 'jump' or radioactive decay, may appear to be random and yet have a cause that has not yet been discovered. For such an event to be completely uncaused belies the 'preferences' that electrons are known to exhibit for filled energy 'shells' in the atom as well as their tendency to always revert to ground state. A totally uncaused quantum event implies some sort of 'free will' on the quantum entity's part, which I find absurd. The recent discovery of non-locality as a fact of life in quantum relationships [see Chapters 9-11] suggests that some causes may be both mysterious and remote, and that absolute randomness is an illusion.

The significance of quantum indeterminacy is something else. It resides in the fact that, in order to predict the future, it is necessary to have complete and accurate knowledge of the present, and that this is information that we cannot have. Heisenberg put it this way: "In the statement, 'If we knew the present in all its details we could predict the future with accuracy' it is the premise rather than the conclusion which is wrong."[24] Because of quantum uncertainty we cannot *as a matter of principle* "know the present in all its details". Our predictions will always be probabilistic rather than deterministic in nature. It is classical predictability, not causality as such, that is denied by quantum theory.

Quantum uncertainty, arising out of quantum discreteness, means the future is unpredictable because the present is unknowable. But science has always proceeded on the assumption that by studying the past we *can* know the present and thus predict the future. The Uncertainty Principle underlying orthodox quantum theory dramatically illustrates just how much of a 180 degree turn physics has made away from traditional scientific ways of thinking. What is the use, then, of studying the past if the present is uncertain and the future unpredictable? Quantum physics gives a very strange answer to this question. We make our inherently uncertain knowledge of the present *actual* by *observation*. It is only when we measure or 'observe' an event that it becomes 'real'. Until then it is only one of a number of potential events which hang suspended as if in a ghost field [Einstein's *Gespensterfeld*] waiting to happen. But what 'triggers' the actualization of quantum events, and why does 'triggering' produce *this* reality and not another? Herein lies the grand dilemma of quantum theory, which no one has yet been able to solve, and which accounts for the multiplicity of interpretations of the theory. The *Copenhagen Interpretation*, with its 'ghostly' potentialities, is the dominant, but not the only, dogma. There is also the *Many Worlds* (Parallel Universes) interpretation, which has a strong minority following; Wheeler's *Participatory Universe;* Chew's *Bootstrap;* Von Neumann's *Observer Consciousness* theory; and a number of others. The most convincing, to my mind, is David Bohm's *Implicate Order*, with its notion of a non-local Quantum Potential, to which I will be devoting considerable analysis later. All of these represent serious attempts to come to terms with quantum 'reality', but none has been entirely accepted by all physicists.

In subsequent chapters I will show you why science is not necessarily the royal road to truth that the hoi polloi often imagine it to be by exploring some of these different interpretations. We shall see how another great physicist, Erwin Schrödinger, found a totally different approach to quantum physics than Heisenberg's, yet came up with the same answers. We shall see how this underscored the paradox of quantum dualism [the wave/particle puzzle], why Bohr opted for *Complementarity*, why Einstein rebelled, how David Bohm reformulated quantum theory using de Broglie's old "pilot wave" notion, and how John Bell, some thirty years after the famous Bohr-Einstein confrontations, found a way out of the difficulties. It is a marvelous tale which, as I have already hinted, traces a mysterious loop from classical continuity and certainty to quantum discreteness and uncertainty and back again to the notion of an undivided wholeness of all things. If this exercise teaches us anything, it is that the pursuit of scientific knowledge is only one road among many to help us decide what is important and relevant for our lives. The lesson is clear that *no* scientific theory, however useful or successful it may have shown itself to be in the past, can be a complete description of the world as it is or as it appears to be. But let me not be too anxious to anticipate my conclusions. There is still a great deal of ground to cover, and I hope that the reader will be as eager to explore it as I am to tell him about it.

SEVEN

WAVE MECHANICS AND QUANTUM MYSTERY

"Neither wave nor particle,
but wave *and* particle."
–*Louis de Broglie*

The contemporary English physicist, F. David Peat, has propounded a theory that events in life are sometimes rather inexplicably synchronous, that is, they cluster together in time in patterns which, though apparently unrelated, appear mysteriously significant to certain observers. Peat's 1987 book *Synchronicity: The Bridge Between Matter and Mind* contains a fascinating discussion of such synchronicities and their possible relevance to science, a few of which, such as Jung's scarab, have become rather celebrated in the telling.[25] The joint discovery of virtually identical theories of evolution by Darwin and Wallace and the almost simultaneous formulation of three separate and distinct theories of the quantum by Heisenberg, Schrödinger, and Dirac in the mid-twenties perhaps also belong in this category.

Whether synchronicity is real or only imagined, it is a fact that, while the young Heisenberg was occupied with his matrix algebra approach to quantum theory, another brilliant physicist, Erwin Schrödinger, was grappling with many of the same problems. Schrödinger's approach, however, was radically different.

Schrödinger was much more concerned with visualizing what goes on inside the atom. He was less of an abstract thinker than Heisenberg, and the theory of the quantum he developed was one that retained many of the aspects of the old classical physics. Schrödinger had been heavily influenced both by Einstein and by Prince Louis Victor de Broglie, who in his doctoral thesis had advanced a theory of 'matter' waves—subsequently experimentally confirmed—that appealed greatly to Schrödinger's intuition. Schrödinger seized on de Broglie's concept of 'waves' of matter, in their behavioral aspects akin to waves of light, in order to see if he could find a 'classical' explanation for the atom's stability, one that would obviate any need for "these damned quantum jumps."

What he came up with was a theory of *wave mechanics* wholly different in concept from Heisenberg's matrices but ultimately equivalent in terms of its mathematical results. It had been Heisenberg's intention to develop a theory that would explain what he termed the atom's "observables", that is, the frequencies, amplitudes, and polarizations of its spectral lines—the atom's 'fingerprint'—without having to rely on such classical notions as position or momentum, which he believed to be in principle unobservable. Schrödinger, on the other hand, because he could see no physical basis for quantum 'jumps', favored a *continuum* theory in which the particle (electron) was visualized as a sort of *Schaumkamm* (whitecap) riding the crest of an all-pervasive electromagnetic wave, or wave 'packet'. Nothing was 'orbiting' in Schrödinger's theory, so that there was no need for quantum jumps. The wave function, represented by a differential equation now universally known as *Schrödinger's Equation*, was all-in-all. The problem was that the wave function represented by the Schrödinger equation, though supposedly descriptive of a classical reality, was not itself physically 'real'. It was a mathematical expression which, as was pointed out to Schrödinger by Max Born, existed in a multidimensional or multi-configurational space. What it described, said Born, were "waves of probability" in configuration space, not real waves in a four-dimensional space-time continuum. Schrödinger's equation gave the *probabili-*

ty of a particle's being found at a particular time and location in space but could not be said to be an exact description of the particle's *actual* path or behavior. This alone, argued Born, disqualified Schrödinger's theory as 'realistic', which was the aspect of his theory that Schrödinger had been most anxious to preserve. What is ironic about all this is that Schrödinger's wave mechanics, though it could not explain the classical conundrums it had been intended to address, has nevertheless become the technician's instrument of choice in 'doing' operational quantum mechanics. Schrödinger's wave mechanics, and Schrödinger's Equation, have won the day against both the Heisenberg and Dirac versions of quantum theory as a laboratory tool for calculating quantum probabilities.

Schrödinger was clearly discomfited by Born's criticisms and by the fact that two theories so antithetical in concept as his and Heisenberg's could yield the identical theoretical result. Heisenberg's theory was based on the supposed reality of the electron as a particle, Schrödinger's on its supposed reality as a wave. But which of the two was it 'really'? Or could it be both at the same time? The answer Bohr later gave was that it could not; the apparent wave/particle duality of the electron represented two complementary aspects of its nature, depending on what experiments were performed. When one performed an experiment to demonstrate the electron's discrete nature, it behaved as a particle; when one performed an experiment to show the electron's wave nature, the electron duly obliged by behaving as a wave. But in Bohr's view it was meaningless to ask what the electron actually *was*. In Heisenberg's words, what we see when we do an experiment on the electron is not nature itself, but "nature exposed to our method of questioning."[26] We never really see the electron as a 'naked' object. The electron's dual nature was apparently inextricably interwoven with the reality of the quantum world...assuming, of course, that there *was* some underlying reality in that world!

The most famous experiment illustrating the electron's dual nature was one that Thomas Young performed in 1803, known as the *two-slit experiment*. Although Young's original experiment dealt with light waves, it is equally valid for so-called 'matter' waves, that is, for all material subatomic entities. In Young's original experiment a beam of light is focused on an opaque screen in which two narrow slits have been cut, so that light which penetrates these slits can be observed at a second screen, serving as a monitor, situated at some distance beyond the first. When the two screens have been set up in this way and a beam of light is allowed to penetrate the first screen [from a light source directly in front of it], what we observe on the monitoring screen is a physical phenomenon, called diffraction, resulting from wave interference. The diffraction pattern is one of alternating light and dark bands of illumination. Such a pattern is typically produced when a series of waves coming from different angles, as from the two separated slits in the first screen, coalesces again on the other side before impacting the monitor. When two wave crests arrive simultaneously from the double slits, they reinforce one another, producing a bright patch on the monitor. But when a wave crest arrives together with a wave trough, the two effects cancel, producing a dark patch. This phenomenon of wave interference is familiar to anyone who has ever observed the play of waves on an ocean beach. Water waves coming together again after meeting an obstruction produce alternate patches of calm and turbulence, corresponding to the alternating dark and bright bands of light on the monitoring screen.

Now, in the two-slit experiment with light (or with electrons) a remarkable thing happens. It is a thing that, in Richard Feynman's words, is "impossible, *absolutely* impossible, to explain in any classical way." What happens, he says, is a "mystery". "Do not keep saying to yourself, if you can possibly avoid it, 'But how can it be like that?', because you will go 'down the drain' into a blind alley from which no one has yet escaped."[27]

What is this remarkable thing that happens? It is that the diffraction pattern, supposedly the result of wave after wave crashing into one another after penetrating the screen, continues to show up on the monitor even when the photon or electron gun which is our power source is slowed down enough so that *only single pho-*

tons or electrons are arriving at the monitor one at a time. It doesn't matter how long the interval between their arrival or whether a thousand photon guns are shooting only one photon at a time through the screen at a thousand different locations around the world. A diffraction pattern *still* builds up, over time, when all these individual results are cumulated. Yet, if one slit is not open, or is suddenly closed, the diffraction pattern *immediately vanishes.* It also vanishes if we try to observe, by means of measuring devices placed at each slit, *which* of the two slits the photon has penetrated. In other words, a diffraction pattern is evidenced whenever we are not looking to see where the photon went and it immediately vanishes when we peek, regardless of whether we send the photons through the two slits *en masse* or singly, at widely separated intervals of time! Observation destroys the effect. All we *ever* see on the monitor is single photons arriving, one at a time, at a specific location, as evidenced by a tell-tale click of a Geiger counter or a scintillating flash of light on a phosphorescent screen. The photons arrive like a hail of bullets, but they build up to a diffraction pattern which, so far as we know in nature, can only be produced by waves.

The mystery is how the photon can be both wave and particle at the same time. How can a single photon 'interfere with itself'? How does it 'know' whether one or both slits are open? If only one slit is open the photon is free to go anywhere it chooses—the whole screen is evenly illuminated. But if both slits are open—if it doubles its options—its choices are restricted; it can *never* go to the dark patches.

I can do no better than to quote John Gribben's description of the mystery:

> "In the experiment with two holes the interference can be interpreted as if the electron that leaves the gun vanishes once it is out of sight and is replaced by an array of ghost electrons each of which follows a different path to the detector screen. The ghosts interfere with one another, and when we look at the

way electrons are detected by the screen we then find the traces of this interference, even if we deal with only one 'real' electron at a time. However, this array of ghost electrons only describes what happens when we are not looking; when we look, all of the ghosts except one vanish, and one of the ghosts solidifies as a real electron. In terms of Schrödinger's wave equation, each of the 'ghosts' corresponds to a wave, or rather, a packet of waves, the waves that Born interpreted as a measure of probability. The observation that crystalizes one ghost out of the array of potential electrons is equivalent, in terms of wave mechanics, to the disappearance of all of the array of probability waves except for one packet of waves that describes one real electron. This is called the 'collapse of the wave function', and bizarre though it is, it is at the heart of the *Copenhagen Interpretation*...(which) depends explicitly on the assumption that myriad ghost particles interfere with each other all the time and only coalesce into a single real particle as the wave function collapses during an observation. What's worse, as soon as we *stop* looking at the electron, or whatever we are looking at, it immediately splits up into a new array of ghost particles, each pursuing its own path of probabilities through the quantum world. Nothing is real unless we look at it, and it ceases to be real as soon as we stop looking."[28]

John Gribben has called this "the central mystery of the quantum world," adding that "There is no clearer example of the interaction of the observer with the experiment." I don't know if Gribben actually believes in ghosts, but it is clear that Einstein didn't. His well-known whimsy once elicited from him the comment that he doubted whether a mouse could bring about a drastic change in the universe merely by looking at it, to which Hugh

Everett, one of the founders of the *Many Worlds* theory, replied that, in his view, the universe was not changed by the mouse's observation—only the mouse was affected.

The mathematics of the two-slit experiment are as follows: Let the statistical distribution of particles on the monitor be represented by a bell-like curve that we shall call A for the case when only slit "A" is open and by a curve that we may call B when only slit "B" is open. If quantum entities did not possess wave-like attributes but, instead, behaved like bullets (to use the Feynman analogy) as they passed through each slit singly, the distribution of bullet-like particles on the monitor when both slits are open would then correspond to a simple addition of the distribution patterns when each slit is open separately. That is, the combined pattern, C, would be simply A+B. This would represent the total *number* of bullet-particles arriving at the monitor or, alternatively, the combined *amplitude* of the separate distribution patterns.

The mysterious wave/particle duality of quantum entities passing through the double slits, however, results in a distinctly *different* distribution curve on the monitor when both slits are open, even though the patterns are the same as for bullets when only one slit at a time is open. The combined curve can no longer be expressed as a simple addition of the patterns for slit "A" and slit "B" separately. The square of a wave's amplitude is a measure of its energy or intensity. "Mathematically", writes John Gribben, "instead of finding that the intensity of both holes together is the sum of their two separate intensities [the sum of the squares], it turns out to be the square of the sum of the two amplitudes."[29] In the above example, therefore, the intensity of the combined wave [both slits open] is not given by $A^2+B^2 = C^2$ but by $(A+B)^2 = C^2$, an expression which, when expanded, is seen to contain an extra term, namely 2AB, which is the 'interference term'. Allowing for the fact that the A's and B's can be negative or positive, this "precisely explains the peaks and troughs in the interference pattern."

The two-slit experiment clearly shows that a quantum entity, such as an electron, is neither a wave nor a particle, but, in the words of Louis de Broglie "both wave *and* particle." Although

Schrödinger's wave mechanics correctly calculated the probabilities of finding the particle in the wave, it shed no light on the "machinery", in Feynman's quaint phrase, that was responsible for the electron's hide-and-seek act. "Nobody knows any machinery", Feynman declared. He believed it impossible to design any apparatus whatever capable of determining the path of the electron through the two slits that will not at the same time destroy the interference pattern:

> "If you have an apparatus which is capable of telling which hole the electron goes through...then you can say that it either goes through one hole or the other. It does; it always is going through one hole or the other—when you look. But when you have no apparatus to determine through which hole the thing goes, then you cannot say that it goes through one hole or the other. To conclude that it goes either through one hole or the other is to produce an error in prediction... The question is how it can come about that when the electrons go through hole No. 1 they will be distributed one way, when they go through hole No. 2 they will be distributed another way, and yet when both holes are open you do not get the sum of the two."[30]

David Bohm, in his classic work *Quantum Theory*, first published in 1951, did manage, I think, to shed some additional light on the matter. His first notable conclusion, which appears obvious after it has been stated, is that "...Since the electrons clearly come through the slit system separately and independently, the interaction between electrons cannot cause the interference pattern." He next notes that, whenever an observation on the system is made, *some* sort of interaction takes place between the electrons and the observing apparatus, and that "The effect of any kind of force of interaction...is to modify Schrödinger's Equation", an idea that led him, a few years later, to reformulate the concepts of wave mechanics to include the notion of a *Quantum Potential*. The impact of measuring apparatus on quantum system results in what is "effectively a transformation of the electron from a wave-like to a particle-like object ... Because the electron continually interacts with many different kinds of systems, each of which develops different potentialities, the electron will undergo continual transformations between its different possible forms of behavior (i.e. wave or particle)." In his book *Quantum Theory* it is obvious that Bohm does not completely share the Copenhagen view. Bohm does not, for example, deny a real existence to the electron prior to observation, nor does he believe that the consciousness of an observer or the presence of a measuring apparatus is required to verify either aspect of its dual nature.[31]

Despite the major contribution of wave mechanics toward improving our understanding of sub-atomic phenomena, the essential mystery of what goes on inside the atom 'in reality' and how the 'machinery' works remains to this day unanswered. Schrödinger's wave mechanics represents the 'machinery' rather more concretely than Heisenberg's matrices or Dirac's abstract mathematical formalism, but the relationship of all three approaches to physical 'reality' remains obscure. No one was more aware of this than Schrödinger himself, who was particularly upset by the 'spin'—to employ a currently popular political term—that the Copenhagenist camp had put on his own theory. He found himself totally out of sympathy with the view that nothing is real until it is measured, and in his famous "cat" paradox he found a dramatic device to illustrate the point. This and other considerations leading to Einstein's famous EPR challenge to Bohr and his Copenhagenist colleagues will form the subject of the next chapter.

EIGHT

SCHRÖDINGER'S CAT AND ALL THAT

"Well, I've often seen a cat without a grin," thought Alice, "but a grin without a cat! It's the most curious thing I ever saw in all my life!"
–Lewis Carroll,
Alice in Wonderland

There is a modern-day paradox, not quite as famous as Zeno's, but justly celebrated among physicists for the stark and dramatic incisiveness with which it makes its point. It is known as the *Paradox of Schrödinger's Cat,* a mythical beast which somehow hangs suspended forever between life and death until someone checks to see which is the case. Schrödinger devised the paradox (after a similar one of Einstein's) to show up the absurdity of the Copenhagen Interpretation of quantum theory, with its 'ghostly' array of superimposed collapsing quantum states. *Schrödinger's Cat* zeroes in on the 'machinery', to use Feynman's colorful term, by which the electron in the two-slit experiment manages to be two things at once—a wave when one is not looking and a particle when one is. But before I tell you about the paradox itself, still unresolved after sixty years of furious debate, it may be helpful to examine a bit more closely some basic concepts.

The 'machinery' behind the two-slit experiment attesting to the electron's dual nature was indeed a curious thing. The electron's

Jekyl and Hyde act was incomprehensible in terms of classical mechanics. The electron behaved one way when it was observed and in another totally different way when unobserved. Schrödinger attempted to resolve this difficulty by substituting a purely wave interpretation for the electron's duality, a wave interpretation in which the wave function represented the amplitudes of a pulsating electromagnetic field. In Schrödinger's theory the electron was initially conceived to be a single wave, but this subsequently became a wave 'packet' because of the inherent theoretical spreading of a single wave through all of space. A wave 'packet', on the other hand, can be confined to as small a region of space as one chooses, so that the electron, when observed, is always found to be within a rather well-defined region.[32] The wave 'packet' exists in what is known as a *superposition* of states, inasmuch as it is a combination of waves which are added together, or superimposed, to give a new totality. As such, the superposition can appear quite irregular, with large spikes of amplitude in places where waves with the same phase have interfered constructively together. At such "image points", to use Schrödinger's phrase, the intensity or energy of the combined wave packet is very large. In Schrödinger's view the wave's particle nature was manifested in such "image points", which moved along with the wave packet, tracing an identifiable trajectory through time and space, a trajectory that was, in fact, made 'visible' in cloud chambers. When such a wave packet was confined within an atom, it corresponded to the standing wave patterns of a vibrating violin string, and the transitions of energy from one atomic level to another—Bohr's quantum 'jumps'—occurred whenever the string's harmonics were sounded. In Schrödinger's pioneering paper on wave mechanics, published in the *Annalen der Physik* in January, 1926, the inventor of wave mechanics suggested that the stability of the atom's energy levels emerged "in the same natural way as the integers specifying the number of nodes in a vibrating string." Schrödinger viewed the atom's transitions of energy not as discrete and abrupt but as smooth and continuous, a conception altogether different from that yielded by Heisenberg's matrices. Most astonishing of all, perhaps, was the fact that two physical theories addressing the same phenomena could be so absolutely at variance with one another and yet yield fundamentally the same theoretical result. The inherent appeal of Schrödinger's wave mechanics over Heisenberg's matrices was due in no small measure to the ability of physicists to visualize a process that in matrix mechanics was expressible only in abstruse mathematical terms.

Schrödinger's description, nevertheless, had its limitations. It was, in fact, not a string that was vibrating in Schrödinger's conception but a collection of harmonically tuned wave disturbances in an electromagnetic field. Whether or not this actually corresponded to an underlying physical reality was problematical. As Born had pointed out to Schrödinger, his theory was visualizable only for the simplest of atomic entities, the hydrogen atom, where only a single electron was involved; for an atom of two electrons a six-dimensional space would be needed, and three more dimensions would be required for each additional electron. This was enough to shatter any interpretation of the theory as having a one-to-one correspondence with any underlying physical reality. Schrödinger acknowledged these criticisms, as well as others, but persisted in clinging to his wave equation, which indeed worked beautifully so far as the mathematics were concerned. Those mathematics were expressed in a rather complex equation which can be compressed to the form $i\hbar\psi = H\psi$ only at the cost of eviscerating it of any detailed consideration of its terms.[33] Such a description lies beyond the scope of this book and is for our purposes unnecessary. Suffice it to say that the Schrödinger Equation, though it looks simple enough, is a complicated expression of a differential equation that relates the rate of change over time of a quantum system to its energy. It conceives of quantum processes in terms of an energy continuum, not in terms of the discrete quantized energy 'jumps' popularized by the views of Bohr and Heisenberg. Despite its radical mathematical and conceptual differences from the views of the Copenhagenist camp, and its inability to address such classical dilemmas as black body radiation and the photoelectric effect, it has proven of immense practical value as a laboratory tool in the application of quantum principles to the development of modern technology. There is not a single instance to date in which its predictions have been proven wrong. That has to say *something* about the validity of Schrödinger's wave mechanics, but exactly what that something is remains, almost seventy years later, a matter of considerable dispute.

Schrödinger himself was severely distressed by the contradictions in his theory, as became apparent when he fell ill, following rather heated discussions with Bohr, while a guest in Bohr's home in 1926. Bohr resolutely defended his conception of the atom as a quantized, albeit abstract, reality, while Schrödinger forcibly argued for his continuum theory. It was during this visit that Schrödinger delivered himself of his oft-quoted remark: "You surely must understand, Bohr, that the whole idea of quantum jumps necessarily leads to nonsense... If we are still going to have to put up with these damned quantum jumps, I am sorry that I ever had anything to do with quantum theory."[34]

Schrödinger's point: If electron waves were not real, but only "waves of probability" in configuration space—in short, if there was no underlying reality to the continuum—then how could the theory of wave mechanics be said to have advanced our knowledge of actual physical processes which were going on at the sub-atomic level?

The Bohr-Heisenberg view of the wave packet, which has become the standard one notwithstanding Schrödinger's objections, is that the superposition of states from which such a wave packet is constructed is only a mathematical expression that defines a *range of probabilities* for the electron to be found within a certain region of space when a measurement is made. This range is defined by the *square* of the wave function. The regions of greatest probability correspond with regions where the wave packet's amplitudes are greatest. Sometimes the electron will actually be found there and will register as a Geiger counter click, while at other times it will not. The probabilities for it to be found at any specific location can be precisely calculated from the square of the wave amplitudes, but whether it will actually be found 'here' rather than 'there' can be determined only on direct observation. Whenever an observation is made, all the 'ghost' possibilities represented by the wave function amplitudes are said to "collapse"; mathematically, the wave function is said to become linear. The question is, were these other possibilities at any time *real* or only *ghosts?* Orthodox quantum theory replies that they are 'real ghosts', with a mathematical chance that any of them might, on observation, have been 'promoted' from the status of 'ghosts' to realities. The existence of the electron at a particular location is only *potential*, says the Copenhagen Interpretation, until someone, somewhere, takes a measurement, whereupon one of these *potentia* becomes 'real'. Until then they exist only in the form of a *superposition*—a combination—of abstract quantum states.[35]

All of this was too much for Schrödinger, who devised his famous "cat" paradox to illustrate the absurdity of the situation. There was clearly something very odd going on. Either the wave function collapse was real, or it was only in the mathematics. But if it was only in the mathematics, then why did the diffraction pattern on the screen vanish when any attempt to observe it was made? What remained was only an irridescent flash on the screen. But why *this* flash in *this* location rather than another? Pure chance, said the Copenhagenists. Nonsense, retorted the opposition, represented chiefly by de Broglie, Schrödinger, and Einstein. It was not possible, they insisted, that a process which was not itself real could produce real effects. If there was no one-to-one correspondence with the physical reality, then what on earth was the theory 'explaining'?

In Schrödinger's opinion the Copenhagen Interpretation [supported chiefly by Bohr, Heisenberg, Pauli, Dirac, and Jordan] was not 'explaining' anything. Its total lack of credibility could be illustrated by the following 'thought experiment'.

Imagine, said Schrödinger, a cat in a sealed box. In the box are also a vial of poison and a bit of radioactive substance with a known probability of releasing, on average, one atom every hour. Attached to this device is a hammer which shatters the vial of poison whenever an atom is released, thereby killing the cat. There is thus a 50% probability that, if we open the box after exactly one hour, the cat will be found to be either alive or dead. The probabilities are equal.

Seen quantum mechanically, however, the situation is different. Quantum mechanically the cat is a collection or ensemble of wave functions which correspond to its individual quantum particles. This holds also for the radioactive substance, the poison, the hammer—indeed, for the entire experiment. According to the Copenhagen Interpretation of the wave function, the whole system exists in a superposition of possibilities which are indefinite until one looks inside the box, that is, until an observation is made. The quantum wave function describing the total system is ambiguous with respect to the "aliveness" or "deadness" of the cat until a measurement is taken, that is, until the box is opened. It is not that the cat is *either* alive or dead prior to an inspection but that it is *both!* Copenhagen orthodoxy regards the wave function of the system as "collapsing" only when the box is opened and the actual state of the cat enters the consciousness of an observer. Only at this point does one of the superimposed possibilities describing the cat's condition become *real*. Prior to this the cat's state might be described as being one of suspended animation.

Now, this conclusion strikes the ordinary person as preposterous, but to some theoretical physicists counting the number of angels that can dance on the head of a pin it is a real conundrum. The best 'solution' to the cat paradox that I have seen is one given by David Bohm, who has reformulated the Schrödinger Equation so as to rid it of its ambiguities [although he may have introduced others in so doing]. It is Bohm's position, which I shall describe in detail later, that the assumption of an actual collapse of the wave function is what lies at the root of the difficulty. Bohm has written: "In our approach...the paradox (of Schrödinger's cat) does not arise because we go beyond the assumption that the wave function provides the most complete possible description of reality."[36] In Bohm's reformulated theory the wave function does not collapse. Collapse is avoided by introducing the notion of a *Quantum*

Potential, a new force which guides a real particle at all times in a manner to simulate its wave nature. I shall have a good deal more to say about Bohm's views in Chapter 13.

The Copenhagen Interpretation of the wave function which inspired Schrödinger to dramatize its weaknesses by means of his famous *cat paradox* actually goes far beyond the simple denial of any physical counterpart to the mathematics of quantum theory. The Copenhagen Interpretation asserts unequivocally that no quantum phenomenon is a real phenomenon until a measurement has been made. It leaves unanswered the question of whether such a measurement requires a human observer. It was Bohr's view that quantum entity and measuring apparatus were all part of an inseparable quantum system, each interacting with the other, and that it was therefore impossible to speak of the objective existence of a quantum entity when it was not being observed. A quantum entity, said Bohr, simply did not *have* any dynamic attributes, such as position and momentum, until a measurement had been made on it, at which point the wave function that 'described' it was viewed as "collapsing" from a multitude of probabilities into some definite 'reality'. Until then, as already indicated, it represented only a *superposition* of different quantum states, each with a different mathematical probability of being 'realized'. John von Neumann had attempted to pinpoint the place or time in the process where the so-called "collapse" occurred, finally concluding that it could only occur in the human consciousness. This, however, begged the question of *whose* consciousness, that is, with which observer did the chain end? Did the universe not exist before there was someone around to observe it? The question seems absurd, but physicists of the stature of John Wheeler have asserted that observer participation plays a vital role in creating the *past* which we observe in the cosmos today.

The fundamental question, it seems, is at what point does the quantum uncertainty and superposition of states that attaches to any quantum system—according to the Copenhagen Interpretation—become a certainty on the human, or cat, level, since the quantum wave function which attaches to any experiment applies to the entire system. This is, in another form, the same question that Einstein addressed to his biographer, Abraham Pais, with respect to the reality of the moon's existence. In the view of many physicists, as well as my own, *Schrödinger's Cat Paradox* effectively destroys the notion of a *Gespensterfeld* surrounding the electron and quashes the idea that only an act of observation, human or otherwise, can "collapse" the wave function, thereby creating an objective reality where none existed before. The *Paradox of Schrödinger's Cat* returns the reality argument to the only arena that has so far withstood the test of time, the arena of mathematics, where no interpretation is needed. Yet in a deeper sense we feel, quite rightly, that mathematics is only a form of shorthand, another language if you will, for giving expression to a deeper underlying physical reality which mere words cannot convey. If there is nothing behind the mathematical facade—if there is no wizard behind the curtain—then what meaning can the equations possibly have? What is it, in Stephen Hawking's arresting phrase, that "breathes fire into the equations" and creates the flesh and blood reality that we personally experience as our own? We intuitively feel that a mathematical equation which gives us results that we can pragmatically employ to enhance our technology and our material well-being must have *some* relevance to a real world. This was, in fact, one of Einstein's deepest convictions, and it was what led him to confront Bohr and his colleagues with another famous 'thought experiment' known as EPR [Einstein, Podolsky, Rosen] in the same year, 1935, in which Schrödinger had devised his "cat" paradox. It is to this experiment and its far-reaching implications for the subsequent development of twentieth century physics that we now turn.

NINE

THE EPR PARADOX: IS REALITY NON-LOCAL?

"I cannot seriously believe in spooky
actions at a distance."
–Albert Einstein

P erhaps the best way to introduce the EPR experiment is to begin with Einstein's theory of relativity and Einstein's concept of causality.

Einstein's famous theory of relativity, as every student of physics knows, assumes the constancy of the speed of light in a vacuum. This assumption has been verified as correct in every experiment devised to test it, and it is now accepted as one of the universal 'givens'. The assumption describes a universe in which events in time and space are seen as relative to an observer's frame of reference, and not as having an independent and objective validity of their own. Because the speed of light is, nevertheless, finite, no two observers not equidistantly situated from an event will record that event as happening *simultaneously*. If we take the argument to an extreme, no two observers *ever* see things happening in quite the same way. In our local world, however, such minute discrepancies of observation can be practically disregarded, because the immense velocity at which light travels overwhelms all other considerations, so that all of our clocks are, in effect, synchronized. We can pretty much all agree that we live in the *same* world because the speed of light (and therefore our awareness of what is going on) is so vast relative to our undertakings.

Though the speed of light is enormous [approximately 300,000 kms/ sec], the fact that it is not infinite is, as one wag has put it, what keeps everything from happening all at once! It is the finiteness of the speed of light that gives us our sense of time. It is what gives our universe its aspect of *local* reality. Now, local reality is an expression with which you may not be well acquainted, but it underlies all of our laws of physics and it is at the heart of the Bohr-Einstein conflict. In a local reality universe there can be no causal connection between events that lie outside of the areas of space-time swept out by one another's light cones.[37] What this means, quite simply, is that if one event occurs somewhere in the universe, say, in a far-flung galaxy, and another event occurs on the Earth, neither can be the cause of the other if the distance separating them is greater than the distance a beam of light could travel in the interval between their occurrence. Local reality means that causal connections between events widely separated in time and space *cannot be instantaneous* because no signal traveling between them can be instantaneous. Even light takes time to go from 'here' to 'there'. To assert that there may be a causal link between two widely-separated events that lie outside of each other's light cones contradicts the assumptions of relativity theory—or so Einstein maintained. Such a causal connection is simply not "reasonable", he insisted, and should therefore be rejected. This was the famous conclusion of the EPR paper.[38]

Bohr disagreed. It was Bohr's contention that quantum entities and the measuring instruments used to observe them form an inseparable, unanalyzable quantum whole and that once such entities have been in "phase entanglement" they will forever after exhibit relational attributes no matter how distantly they may be spatially separated. Bohr's view of quantum reality was a *holistic* one in which observed quantum events were to be regarded as some sort of emergent unity encompassing both particle and observer. It was a view that was anathema to Einstein, who remained a realist to the bitter end.

What bothered Einstein most about the quantum orthodoxy that emerged from Copenhagen was its air of unreality. Einstein could not accept that quantum events, such as orbital 'jumps', happen without cause, or that the observer may 'create' the reality he sees. Ironically, Einstein's own theory of relativity was also, in a sense, observer-dependent. Einstein believed in what is known as *local realism*. He believed in the independent existence of a real universe that went on 'ticking' whether there was anyone around to witness it or not. He had once commented that he did not believe that a mouse, simply by looking at the universe, could change it, and he was convinced that the moon was 'really there' whether one was observing it or not. In short, Einstein's was a common sense kind of universe with which most of us would feel comfortable even though we might not be able to relate to some of its more bizarre relativistic aspects.

Bohr and his colleagues, on the other hand, kept insisting that there was a fundamental indeterminacy to the universe, not just because the Heisenberg Uncertainty Principle made it impossible to "know the present in all its details", but because, to strict constructionists like Bohr, there *was* no present to be known until someone, somewhere, took a 'reading' of it. It was like saying that a room—or a person—had no temperature until a thermometer was brought in to measure it. Perhaps, more accurately, what the true believers in the Copenhagen orthodoxy were saying was that there was a *multiple range* of temperatures, represented in quantum theory by the Schrödinger wave function, which only existed as *potentia* until a measurement was taken. One of these temperatures then became 'real' as the wave function representing the alternative probabilities 'collapsed' into linearity. Theory did not say, however, nor could it, at what point in this sequence of events the potential became real nor why the particular 'reality' that emerged was chosen.

The stage was clearly set for a grand experiment.

Einstein threw down the gauntlet in a paper jointly written with the assistance of two colleagues, Boris Podolsky and Nathan Rosen, that appeared in the May, 1935, issue of *Physical Review*. Its title was simply: *"Can quantum-mechanical description of physical reality be considered complete?"* Einstein and his colleagues took it as self-evident that, for a physical theory to be considered complete, "Every element of the physical reality must have a counterpart in the physical theory...", and they went on to propose an experiment based on the following premise: *"If, without in any way disturbing a system, we can predict with certainty (that is, with a probability equal to unity) the value of a physical quantity, then there exists an element of physical reality corresponding to this physical quantity."* Thus, said EPR, if we have two quantum systems that are separated in space and we are able to obtain information about one of these systems by means of a measurement on the other, in such a manner that the second system is not disturbed in any way, then there exists an element of physical reality with respect to the second system. Quantum theory denied this, making the physical reality of the second system dependent on a measurement process carried out on the first system. Quantum theory said that the second system *had* no real existence prior to the measurement on the first system. EPR retorted that to make the second system's physical reality dependent on the physical reality of the first system, when there could be no apparent physical (local) connection between them, was absurd and that *"No reasonable definition of reality could be expected to permit this."* The argument therefore came down to what was a "reasonable" definition of reality, and on this the protagonists were unable to reach any agreement.

The actual experiment that Einstein proposed involved the following: Suppose, he said, that we have two electrons initially at rest, in close proximity to one another, so that their phases have become "entangled" and certain of their dynamic attributes have become correlated with one another. If these electrons are then permitted to move apart, the velocity of the one will always be equal and opposite to the velocity of the other, that is, the sum of their individual velocities will be zero. This follows from certain physical principles of angular momentum, and the relationship holds for both classical and quantum systems. If we measure the velocity of one electron and find that it is "X", then it is immediately apparent that the velocity of the second will be "-X". Or we could measure the position of the first and be immediately assured of the position of the second. We are thus able to obtain information about one quantum system which is peculiarly correlated with another system by performing a measurement on the first system which does not disturb the second system in any way. This was Einstein's criterion for reality. It was obvious to Einstein and his colleagues that if information about a quantum entity, in this case, an electron, could be obtained indirectly without there being any question of "disturbance", then *this information must have existed all along*. It must have existed from the time of the initial separation of the two systems, the two electrons, and *could not have been imparted to the second system merely through an act of measurement on the first system*, most assuredly not if the second system were *spatially separated* from the first and perhaps millions of miles away. To argue, as quantum theory did, that such information could be imparted *instantaneously* across space and did not actually *exist* prior to a measurement presupposed some sort of a superluminal signal between the two quantum systems at the time of measurement, a presumption that violated the principle of relativity and the assumption of local realism. Such a presumption, Einstein and his colleagues maintained, was simply not "reasonable".

But what was reasonable in the eyes of one man was not necessarily reasonable in the eyes of the other. *Reasonableness* meant different things to Bohr and to Einstein. Bohr's refutation of EPR, however, was vague and scarcely comprehensible, arguing as it did that it made no sense to speak of the independent reality of two correlated quantum systems. Any such reality, said Bohr, was inextricably entangled with the measuring process. Essentially what was involved was "the question of an influence on the very conditions which define the possible types of predictions regarding the future behavior of the system."[39] This abstruse reply was typical of Bohr's manner of explication and it proved unsatisfactory to Einstein, as it did to many. No further progress was recorded toward resolving the issue until some thirty years later, when John Bell formulated his Inequality Theorem, which Henry Stapp has lauded as one of the most important in physics.

At the root of the dispute between Bohr and Einstein lay the concept of *local realism*. Local realism, or local reality, means that all events have causes, that these causes reside in the known laws of physics, and that the effects of these laws diminish with distance; they do not reach *instantaneously* across the universe. Instantaneous actions at a distance—which Einstein called "spooky"—are impossible because the speed of light is limited. No signal of any sort can be propagated through space any faster than light speed. Therefore, physical influences which originate at any given point in the universe cannot spread out any faster than the light cone from that point and can have no effect on anything which lies outside the area encompassed by this light cone. Quantum theory denied this, in effect insisting that non-local connections existed throughout all of space-time between quantum particles that had once been "phase entangled". This meant that, if the "Big Bang" theory was correct, everything in the universe was literally correlated with everything else!

Let me direct your attention to this curious expression *phase entanglement*. What, exactly, does it mean?

Stripped of its mathematical pretensions, phase entanglement simply means that, where two quantum entities, each represented by a wave function, have interacted and have become correlated, they in effect become part of a single quantum system. The two quantum entities are now part of a single indivisible and unanalyzable whole, and they will remain forever associated with a single wave function even if they separate and wind up in opposite 'corners' of the universe. The wave function which represents them is regarded as 'stretched out' through all of space as a superposition of phantom probabilities until a measurement on one or another of the 'entangled' entities is taken. At that instant the wave function 'collapses' and a single one of this array of phantom attributes becomes 'real'. When this happens, the correlated attribute of its entangled twin becomes instantly 'real' as well, notwithstanding the fact that the two quantum entities may be millions of miles apart. The correlation between them is a result of their once having interacted in close proximity and is not the result of any superluminal signal between them traversing millions of miles of space.

What makes the situation even more curious is the fact that "phase entanglement", supposedly responsible for producing these 'real' effects, is not in itself 'real' in the eyes of those who argue most strongly for it. It is simply a mathematical concept. This is because phase entanglement, which Schrödinger regarded as *the* most salient characteristic of quantum theory, occurs in what is known as *configuration space*, which is a multi-dimensional mathematical space whenever more than one quantum entity is involved and which therefore cannot be visualized as occurring in our familiar three-dimensional world. Yet it is supposed to produce real effects there, effects which, moreover, are not pre-existing but which attain the status of physical reality only when a measurement of some kind is made.

Einstein would not accept this interpretation. He argued that the act of separation of the two quantum entities re-establishes the independent physical reality of each when they move apart. On separation, each is again represented by its own wave function. If they are subsequently found to be correlated, then this correlation *must have existed from the beginning; it cannot have been instantly and mysteriously acquired.* To conclude otherwise would be in violation of the principle of relativity which mandates the constancy of the speed of light. Schrödinger was of the same mind, holding that "measurements on separated systems cannot directly influence each other—that would be magic."[40] The whole EPR debate thus came down to a matter of the fundamental nature of 'reality'. Einstein believed in a local reality;

Bohr and company did not. Bohr's view was a *holistic* one, suggesting that ultimate reality was more than the sum of its parts. Einstein's local reality presupposed the separateness and objectively independent existence of the parts. In Bohr's view the universe was a seamless web of non-local connections, not because superluminal signals might be passing among the parts, but because that was the *nature* of the whole. This was a metaphysical, even a mystical, concept that had no foundation whatsoever in classical physics, or even any good quantum explanation, but it has been an integral insight of the wisdom of the East for thousands of years. To Einstein it was anathema, but subsequent developments in physics suggested strongly that Bohr had come much closer to the truth than Einstein. Reality did appear to be holistic after all, and not just the sum of its parts. However, this only made the land of Oz without a wizard in sight more mysterious and more paradoxical than ever.

Before letting you in on how the paradox was resolved, I want to make a few additional observations.

Einstein's view that quantum theory was "incomplete" was based on the quite understandable assumption that there, in fact, *was* an objectively existing physical reality to be discovered. Einstein had pointed out that such an assumption was the natural fundamental basis of all of physics. Any scientific theory worth its salt *must have some counterpart* in this supposed underlying physical reality. If a scientific theory is not in touch with physical reality, then it cannot be said to further a scientific understanding of how the world works. If quantum theory is simply a mathematical tool that permits us to calculate probabilities but has no real link with the empirical facts, is it really a scientific theory, or is it magic? Magic or not, it is becoming increasingly evident that the world *is* a holistic phenomenon, rather than a mechanical one, and that the reductionist assumptions which have underlain science for hundreds of years are no longer tenable. The real world may not in fact be describable any longer in terms of a scientific model that purports to be a complete counterpart to reality. There may be some truths about it which supersede any supposedly representational theory. Bohr had opined that "There is no quantum world; there is only an abstract quantum physical description", and Einstein throughout his life kept searching for the 'hidden' variables which would complete his theory and restore classical causality. In a sense the whole EPR debate was a non-event in which the protagonists were talking past each other. Einstein was attacking a phantom world of ghostly waves and particles which Bohr denied really existed, while Bohr was defending a notion of 'complementarity' that was incomprehensible to Einstein. Einstein insisted on a realistic accounting for an unreal event, the 'collapse' of the wave function, yet the only collapse which actually occurred was in the mathematics. Thus the central paradox remained: How could a mathematical formalism which accounted so well for the experimental results be completely divorced from reality? Perhaps there was an alternative explanation.

It turns out that there was, and it was called *Many Worlds*, or the *Parallel Universes* interpretation. There are, in fact, a number of alternative quantum interpretations. In the opinion of physicist Nick Herbert, "All of them without exception are preposterous."[41]

Many Worlds has actually quite a strong minority following in physics today. Many physicists who cannot stomach the notion of collapsing wave functions but who, unlike Bohr, require a visual interpretation of quantum reality, have adopted a point of view first proposed by Hugh Everett in the nineteen-fifties and subsequently elaborated and modified by both De Witt and Deutsch. Briefly, the *Many Worlds* theory holds that the Schrödinger wave function does *not* collapse but that *all* of its manifold ghostly probabilities are realized when a measurement is taken. Instead of a single emergent reality a multitude of universes branches off in different directions, each one a slightly different copy of itself. We, however, remain aware of our presence only in this one universe that we jointly inhabit. Feynman's *sum over histories* approach to quantum mechanics is in some respects similar, in that it describes a quantum entity as following *all possible paths* in the atom as it moves from point

"A" to point "B". David Bohm has explained that Everett's theory does not actually postulate the creation of multiple real universes but only of multiple *awarenesses* of a single universe which, nevertheless, are not aware of each other. This may be a fine distinction, but what is clear is that the *Many Worlds* theory does not *per se* solve the riddle of non-locality that was posed by EPR. All it does, in my opinion, is to make an end run around the many difficulties involved in the notion of wave function collapse by substituting an even more outlandish hypothesis in its place.

The *Parallel Universes* theory, I believe, purchases reality at too high a price, and I have given it rather short shrift because, in Einstein's words, "It is too weird to be credible." It violates the principle of Occam's Razor, which is that a scientific theory should not involve a multiplicity of unnecessary assumptions. Oddly enough, some modern cosmologists favor it because they can introduce quantum concepts into their cosmology without having to jettison local physical reality. Are they, in fact, deceiving themselves, or is there more to the notion of *Many Worlds* than meets the eye? I shall have more to say on this later.

A final observation. Bohr reconciled himself to the apparently dual nature of all quantum phenomena, as exemplified in the well-known wave/particle duality of light, by formulating his *Principle of Complementarity*. We cannot pin nature down to a single particular aspect, he said, but we can only obtain a complete picture by including its opposite, or complementary, aspect. Bohr had apparently been influenced in this view by his fascination with Chinese philosophy, as embodied in the concept of T'ai-chi. There is a lot to be said for the concept that opposites define the limits of truth. Certain concepts, such as truth and falsehood, beauty and ugliness, good and evil, or even such physical concepts as long and short, bright and dark, etc., can only be properly appreciated in terms of an awareness of their opposites, even though such awareness may be purely contextual or subjective. The notion of complementarity broadens the picture by introducing the idea of a *range* of differences or gra-

dations between extremes. It gives rise to the concept of diversity, or variety, said to be the spice of life. But to what extent are
such complementary notions as wave and particle an essential
part of the underlying physical 'reality'?

Einstein never felt comfortable with Bohr's concept of complementarity, a concept concerning which he complained he had
never been able to achieve a sharp formulation. In my opinion
the notion of complementarity is a profound one, though its
basis in our perceptions may be more apparent than real.

But Bohr's concept of complementarity could not, in a single
theory, encompass the opposite notions of local realism and of
non-locality in a way that made sense to Einstein. Einstein's was
a *local* universe, and it remained that way to realists of all per-
suasions until John Bell *proved mathematically* that *no* theory of
local realism could ever hope to explain its highly correlated
structure. Quantum theory, on the other hand, did so, and *was*
compatible with such a structure. As John Bell showed, it yielded predictions which lay beyond the ability of any theory of local
realism to achieve. During the 'seventies and 'eighties laboratory
experiments were performed which corroborated the statistical
correlations that quantum theory routinely spewed forth and
which had been the focus of the EPR paradox. The Aspect experiments, in particular, proved that a degree of correlation existed
in the behavior of quantum entities which *significantly exceeded*
that which was permissible under any theory of local realism. It
is a pity that Einstein did not live to see these results, because
they would have been of supreme interest to him. There is little
question but that he would have been forced to accept them,
though he might still have felt "in his bones", as he was wont to
put it, that they did not represent the whole of reality.

I shall discuss the Bell Theorem, which Henry Stapp has
called "the most profound discovery of science", in the next
chapter.[42]

TEN

FOR WHOM THE BELL TOLLS: THE INEQUALITY THEOREM

"Bell's Theorem has shown that the
universe has a non-local aspect."
–F. David Peat

S ome three decades after the great EPR debate a physicist named John Stewart Bell became interested in the profound issues that had been addressed, but left unresolved, by Bohr and Einstein. To Bell's great credit he managed to find an ingenious way to force nature into revealing its hand. Bell asked himself if there was any way to distinguish between local reality and non-local reality theories in terms of their *consequences*. If there was, then it might be possible to do laboratory experiments with respect to such consequences that would tip the hat in favor of one theory or another. In a paper submitted to the journal *Reviews of Modern Physics* in 1964 Bell came up with an answer. Bell found a formula to test Einstein's EPR argument in a manner that the great physicist had not imagined. Conclusive proof—as conclusive as such proof ever gets in physics—did not come, however, until Alain Aspect and colleagues [University of Paris at Orsay] conducted a series of extremely precise experiments in the early 'eighties , experiments in which the superluminal nature of quantum correlations was established beyond a reasonable doubt.

With the publication of Aspect's results in 1982 the bell had truly tolled for the notion of local reality, and a whole new world of metaphysics had opened up.

What, exactly, did John Bell accomplish that was of such earthshaking significance, and how did he do it?

It is not easy, I have discovered, to find a clear and concise description of the Bell Theorem and its import in terms that the lay reader can understand. This is not so much because the theorem itself is complex—it is not—but rather because its derivation requires a rather intimate acquaintance with some of the notions of quantum physics and an appreciation of how these differ from the classical view. Even today there are physicists who dismiss Bell's discovery as 'old hat' and are not greatly disturbed by its implications. Yet these implications, I feel, are profound, for they define the very nature of the kinds of universe that are possible under two very different physical approaches, namely, the quantum and the classical. Equally important, Bell's Theorem shows us a way of distinguishing between them. Bell's conclusions thus point the direction in which physics must go if it is to make further progress toward science's traditional goal of understanding what the world is like and, by implication, making it possible for mankind to benefit from that understanding. In my opinion they also invite exploration of a vast web of metaphysical relationships that bind the universe together, as suggested by the now established scientific fact of non-locality. As Menas Kafatos and Robert Nadeau have put it in their recent book:

> "Simply put, the classical assumption that the collection of parts constitutes the whole has proven invalid...the results of the experiments testing Bell's Theorem suggest that all the parts, or any manifestion of 'being' in the vast cosmos, are seamlessly interconnected in the unity of "Being"... To put it differently, (classical physics) presumed that...one could analyze the whole into parts and deduce the nature of the whole from its parts. With the discov-

ery of non-locality that picture is reversed—it is the whole which discloses ultimately the identity of the parts..."[43]

To which Jim Baggott has added:

"Three centuries of gloriously successful physics have brought us right back to the kind of speculation that it took three centuries of philosophy to reject as meaningless."[44]

Well, then, if the matter is so important, let us see if we cannot get a better fix on what John Bell accomplished.

I have indicated that Bell, an Einstein sympathizer and supporter in the EPR debate, decided to see for himself if the issues of that debate, which had been left more or less in limbo for thirty years, could be clarified in a *testable* manner. These issues came down to whether certain correlations between quantum particles—correlations which both Bohr and Einstein agreed existed—reflected a universal reality that was *local* in nature or one that was *non-local*. Einstein had written: "I cannot seriously believe in the quantum theory because it cannot be reconciled with the idea that physics should represent a reality in time and space, free from spooky actions at a distance."[45] Bohr's view was the exact opposite. Bohr had written: "There is no quantum world; there is only an abstract quantum physical description."[46] Between these two views there was a vast gulf of misunderstanding, which the two antagonists never managed to bridge in their lifetimes. All of physics since Newton had been built on the assumption that everything in the universe could be explained by local action, that is, by forces which operated in a particular neighborhood. These local forces could be summed up in the four basic laws of physics [the strong force, the weak force, electromagnetism, and gravity], whose effectiveness all diminished with distance, and which could not be propagated through space at a speed greater than the maximum velocity of light [300,000 kms/sec]. Einstein himself had declared in his autobiography: "On one supposition we should, in my opinion, absolutely hold fast: The real factual situation [of a physical system] is independent of what is done with another system which is spatially separated from the former." In the famous EPR experiment with Podolsky and Rosen he had affirmed his faith in the reality of a physical system if, without disturbing it in any way, we could predict its attributes by 'interviewing' a second system with which it was correlated, but spatially separated, in the scientific meaning of the term. Quantum theory, on the other hand, made the reality of the first system depend upon a process of measurement carried out on the second system. Quantum theory did not accord the first system *any objective reality* in the absence of a measurement on the other (correlated) system. *"No reasonable definition of reality"*, said Einstein, *"could be expected to permit this."* [italics mine]

The battle lines between Bohr and Einstein, between the classical and the quantum views of how the world worked, were thus drawn by this pregnant phrase of Einstein's concerning "reasonableness". On the issue of what was "reasonable" the debate between the two men foundered, and no further useful discussion between them was possible.

The philosophical gap between Bohr's and Einstein's views of the universe was almost as wide as it could be. Clearly, the principle of local causes had proved valid in many areas of physics, as had been demonstrated over and over again through the centuries. But quantum physics, that twentieth century upstart, was now saying that it did not adequately encompass everything, and that on the quantum level, in particular, it was incomplete. The predictions of quantum theory distinctly implied a non-local principle of action. Was it conceivable that there might also be non-local forces or laws that went beyond both quantum theory and relativity? Was it conceivable that everything in the universe might be distantly connected to everything else in a way that none of us have ever imagined?

The issue, it seems to me, cuts right to the heart of physics, a discipline which has always been fundamentally reductionist in nature, insisting that everything knowable about a physical system can be understood in terms of the functioning of its simplest parts. Scientists since Galileo and Newton have maintained that, if we can understand these parts and how they cooperate together, then we have *by definition* understood everything about the system. Personally, I have never felt this to be so, believing that there are truths about wholes which cannot be derived from the most detailed knowledge of their constituent parts. A common example is water, whose quality of *wetness* is not predictable from a chemical analysis of its two component elements, hydrogen and oxygen. Human consciousness, in my opinion, is an even more striking example. It is clear to me that consciousness is something which is *ontologically distinct* from the brain itself, or the millions of neurons that comprise it, and there are many more examples of this sort in nature. I shall have more to say about this in Chapter 17.

When it comes right down to it, I do not think that the notion that the world of our experience consists of a number of wholes which are ontologically distinct from their parts is a seriously debatable proposition. I think most of us will accept the statement that there are fundamental human experiences and values which *cannot* be reduced to the level of the physical for an explanation of their psychic content and meaning. Ponder, if you will, the fact that physics has nothing whatsoever to say about those matters which are of supreme importance to us as individuals, matters such as love, purpose, fulfillment, recognition, morals, art, music, and companionship—in short, all of the essential matters of the heart that make us human. These things belong to what is known as a *noetic* realm, which includes the mental and the spiritual, in contrast to the things of the material world. None of them, in my opinion, ever stand the slightest chance of being understood via a reductionist analysis, that is, in terms of a local causality theory of the functioning of their simplest constituent parts. But what about the brute material world itself? Is it really a place where nothing *physical* ever happens unless one local force acts directly upon another? Is it conceivable that the physical world itself is also mysteriously interconnected by non-local forces, by "spooky actions at a distance"?

The discoverer of relativity, Albert Einstein, could not imagine it because—according to relativity—no signal can be transmitted through space faster than the speed of light. Therefore there can be no instantaneous connections between spatially separated systems. And therefore the quantum theory, which predicts that such connections exist, must be "incomplete". Or so argued the protagonists of EPR. *Q.E.D.*

The problem was that Bohr, along with other defenders of the quantum faith, did not accept this, and it remained a troublesome issue in the rest of the physics community. After all, quantum mechanics was a 'working' theory and a very successful one at that; its predictions had never failed. Bohr had vaguely replied to the EPR argument in terms that Einstein had found incomprehensible, uttering such opaque phrases as "...there is essentially the question of an influence on the very conditions which define the possible types of predictions regarding the future behavior of the system." What on earth did this mean? It is unfortunate that neither Einstein nor Bohr seems to have focused as penetratingly on the issue of *verification* as John Bell did thirty years later when he succeeded in breaking the impasse between them.

Bell's genius was to find a mathematical formulation that strictly defined the necessary characteristics of every local reality theory. Bell reasoned that, if Einstein was right, and events in spatially separated systems were not causally linked, then it must be possible, somehow, to state this proposition mathematically. If what happened in one region of space was independent of what happened in another region, it must be possible to describe, mathematically, the situation in both regions and systems *as a simple superposition of what happens in them separately. The whole must be expressible as a simple sum of the contributions of its separate and independently existing parts.*

The long shadow of Zeno's paradox of motion is seen in the Bohr-Einstein conflict as well. Is separateness 'real' and, if so, how does the unity of the whole emerge from an aggregation of the parts? Or are both concepts somehow illusions, mental constructs that we have engineered in order to enable us to deal practically with the world?

At this point I think it is important that I nail down what is meant by the phrase "spatial separation" as employed in EPR. Terms such as "space-like separated" and "Einstein separability", which mean the same, are often encountered in the literature. In layman's terminology two events are space-like separated if they happen more quickly than it would take a beam of light to span the distance between them. Strictly speaking, such events would not have to be simultaneous, or instantaneous, they would simply have to occur in such rapid succession that no signal, moving at the speed of light, could travel from the first event to the second before the second occurred. Space-like separated events can occur at any distance. In the Aspect experiments, which finally established the authenticity of Bell's findings, such events were engineered to occur over a distance of only 26 feet, in a physics laboratory, within a time-span of only ten nanoseconds—four times the speed of light—in order to ensure the reliability of the outcome.[47] When two events take place that are space-like separated, their relationship to one another is said to be non-local, because local *means* within the time parameter encompassed by the speed of light. The whole point of Einstein's argument with Bohr, although it was not so specifically stated, was about this issue of *locality*. Einstein maintained that no distant system could be influenced by another if the two were space-like separated, because there would not be enough time for a signal to travel between them. Therefore, what happens at the distant system must be independent of the system which is spatially separated from it, is not "disturbed" by it, in the language of EPR. That system, Einstein argued, must have an independently existing objective reality. No other view of the matter, in Einstein's opinion, was "reasonable".

Bell's contribution toward moving beyond the Bohr-Einstein impasse lay in formulating a mathematical equation that strictly defined the limits of what was locally "reasonable". There are a number of ways to approach the concepts that lie behind the derivation of Bell's Inequality, none of them easy. Bell's Theorem is simple enough, being merely a statement of the (almost) obvious. What is more difficult is to understand the concepts of what actually goes on at the quantum level with respect to such things as electron spin or the polarization of photons. It is not absolutely necessary to know what either "spin" or "polarization" means in order to understand the experiments; physicists themselves do not know what these things 'really' are. But it is necessary to follow through the steps of the experiments carefully to see how the conclusions are reached.

Bell himself parodied his original theme in a published article called *The Case of Dr. Bertlmann's socks.*[48] This parody, I think, gives a helpful introduction to the Bell Theorem. The elements of the parody can be shown to have a precise parallel to the elements of the spin and polarization experiments that I shall describe later.

In this parody John Bertlmann, a research scientist, is conducting wash tests on pairs of new socks to test their durability, along with various other wear characteristics, under varying temperatures. Bertlmann launders a large sample of new socks under different conditions. He launders pairs of socks at temperatures of zero (0) degrees Celsius, 45 degrees, and 90 degrees, giving a pass or fail grade to each sock on each test and comparing the results. Allowing for certain simplifying assumptions concerning substitutability, he finds that the following conclusions can be drawn:

For any large collection of new socks:

(1)   The number that could pass at 0 degrees (test a) but not at 45 degrees (test b)

PLUS

(2)   The number that could pass at 45 degrees (test b) but not at 90 degrees (test c)

IS NOT LESS THAN

(3) The number that could pass at 0 degrees (test a) but not at 90 degrees (test c).

This conclusion Bell termed "trivial", because statements (1) and (2) are readily seen to be subsets of a larger whole (3) which encompasses them both. In the same way, however, statements (1) and (2) also contain subsets, so that when we combine all these subsets into a single expression, an overall inequality can be derived.

Here is the way this is done:

Let "n" be the total number of tests on each sock. Then a shorthand expression for statement (1) might be n[a+, b-], where "a" and "b" are the tests performed and the symbols "+" and "-" indicate success or failure in each test. Similarly, shorthand expressions for statements (2) and (3) would be n[b+, c-] and n[a+, c-], respectively. The expression n[a+, b-] might then be thought of as consisting of two subsets, namely, n[a+, b-, c+] and n[a+, b-, c-], in one of which the individual socks pass test "a", fail test "b", and pass test "c" and in the other of which they pass test "a", fail test 'b", and fail test "c". Thus broken into subsets, statements (1), (2), and (3) can be succinctly summarized in the following manner:

Statement (1) n[a+,b-] = n[a+,b-,c+] + n[a+,b-,c-] (4)
Statement (2) n[b+,c-] = n[a+,b+,c-] + n[a-,b+,c-] (5)
Statement (3) n[a+,c-] = n[a+,b+,c-] + n[a+,b-,c-] (6)

Now, the expression n[a+,b-] of equation (4) is *at least* equal to one of its subsets and can therefore be re-written as an inequality:

$$n[a+,b-] \geq n[a+,b-,c-] \qquad (7)$$

and similarly the expression n[b+,c-] of equation (5) can be re-written as:

$$n[b+,c-] \geq n[a+,b+,c-] \qquad (8)$$

Then by adding inequalities (7) and (8) we get

$$n[a+,b-] + n[b+,c-] \geq n[a+,b-,c-] + n[a+,b+,c-] \quad (9)$$

and substituting from equation (6) we get

$$n[a+,b-] + n[b+,c-] \geq n[a+,c-] \quad (10)$$

This is the expression known as *Bell's Inequality.*

Is this what the fuss is all about, this inoccuous and almost trivial formula? Can this be the greatest discovery in physics?

Well, not the expression itself, but what it stands for. It can be made to stand for the spin of electrons or the polarizations of photons (in addition to such mundane things as socks) and then compared with the predictions of quantum physics. What Bell's Inequality tells us, when quantum entities are substituted for socks, spin detectors or polarization analyzers for washing machines, and angles of orientation in space for wash temperatures, is that there are mathematically definable limits on certain quantum correlations. These limits follow directly from the assumption of local causality embedded in the inequality and can therefore be compared directly with the predictions of quantum theory. When they are thus compared, it turns out that the limits which Bell's Inequality sets on such correlations are *violated* by quantum theory. In other words, quantum theory not only allows but predicts a substantially greater degree of inter-connectedness between quantum entities than Einstein thought "reasonable."

This immediately makes quantum theory, in the words of Karl Popper, "falsifiable". That is, quantum theory can be *tested* to see whether its predictions are correct. If quantum theory passes the test, and its predictions stand, we know at least *that physical reality must be non-local,* because Bell's Theorem proves that no *local* theory can produce all of the same results. That is the essential meaning of Bell's discovery. Bell's Theorem is a tool for resolving the local reality question that was not available either to Bohr or to Einstein when they were conducting their grand debates. If it had been available, one wonders what Einstein might have said, for Einstein was an honest thinker, dedicated to searching out the truth.

Now, let us see how Bell's Theorem can be applied toward resolving the great issues involved in the EPR debate.

The original version of Bell's Theorem involves a consideration of particle 'spin'. Particle spin is not quite the same as the spin of a top, but it is nevertheless a measure of rotation. Particle spin is said to define a *direction in space* for a material particle, a direction described as either "up" or "down" depending on whether the particle's spin is clockwise or counter-clockwise with respect to the axis of measurement.

Particle spin, however, is so abstruse a concept that I have decided to abandon it in attempting to convey to you the essence of Bell's Inequality. Physicists themselves do not know what 'spin' really means, except that it is akin to the reluctance of a spinning top or a turning carousel to slow down. In this it is reminiscent of the property of inertia. Since nothing is actually 'spinning', angular momentum would perhaps be a more accurate term to use.[49]

Suffice it to say that, using the concept of particle spin, the *same* expression [Expression 10, p. 84] for Bell's Inequality can be derived as was obtained in the more homely example of Bertlmann's socks. Note, once again, that this expression is based on the assumption of *local realism*, in which the whole is taken to be the sum of the parts. Quantum theory, however, *violates* Bell's Inequality, because under the rules of quantum math *either of the subsets of Expression 10 can be greater than the whole!* Quantum mechanics comes up with a totally unexpected, and seemingly illogical result, because it does not make the locality assumption. In terms of particle spin, quantum mechanics says that measuring one component of spin *changes the other components* after they have already been measured, so that one of the subsets of Expression 10 *can actually be greater than the other two combined.*

Fortunately, there is another way to approach Bell's Theorem that I have found somewhat easier to grasp. It has to do with the phenomenon called *polarization*, a physical curiousity with which anyone who has ever used polarized sunglasses is at least superficially acquainted.

Polarized sunglasses work by blocking out a portion of the sunlight which reaches the eye through their especially constructed lenses. These lenses are made of a plastic material whose molecules have been elongated to 'line up' in a certain direction. They will transmit only those photons out of any given beam of light which are 'lined up', that is, polarized, in the same direction.

Ordinary sunlight by itself is unpolarized, or rather it is polarized in all directions, because each wave oscillates independently as it moves forward through space. Technically, the direction in space of the oscillations of each individual wave about its axis of transmission constitute its polarization. Polarization is actually the concept of particle spin applied to the photon.

Now, when sunlight strikes the surface of a pair of polarized sunglasses, only those light waves whose polarization is in the same plane as the elongated molecules of the plastic material of the lens will penetrate through to the eyes of the wearer. All of the remaining rays will be blocked out. If then a second piece of plastic is placed directly behind the first and is rotated 90 degrees so that its elongated internal structure is at right angles to the first, *all* of the remaining light is obstructed from reaching the eye, and the blockage will be total.

A helpful way to think about this is in terms of two half-open venetian blinds super-imposed on one another. When both blinds are vertically aligned with one another, 100% of the light which reaches them *and is also vertically aligned* will penetrate both blinds to reach the viewer's eye. When, on the other hand, one of the blinds is horizontal and the other vertical, it is obvious that no light will penetrate.

This illustration has direct relevance to Bell's Theorem and the EPR experiment. In the polarization version of EPR, pairs of photons that have started out from a single quantum state [one in which their net angular momentum is zero] move outward in opposite directions and are then passed through calcite crystals to determine the direction of their polarizations. Behind the crystals are photomultiplier tubes that register the action, counting whether the photons reaching the crystal are polarized in line with its optical axis [which we may call vertical] or are oppositely polarized to it [which we may call horizontal].

Now, both classical and quantum theory agree that pairs of photons which are generated from a single quantum source in this way will be 100% correlated. "Except for the difference in their direction of travel, the photons in each pair are identical twins. If one of them is polarized vertically, the other is also polarized vertically. If one of the photons in the pair is polarized horizontally, the other photon also is polarized horizontally. No matter what the angle of polarization, both photons in every pair are polarized in the same plane."[50] In terms of our homely venetian blind example, this means that if one member of the photon pair passes through the first venetian blind, it will also pass through the second venetian blind 100% of the time, *providing* that both blinds are lined up in the same way. If they are 'crossed', however, this will *not* be the case, particularly if they are crossed at right angles to one another. If they are crossed at right angles, no light will penetrate them, as we saw in the analogy of the sunglasses. The failure of any light to penetrate when the blinds are crossed at right angles is described as 100% *negative* correlation, while the opposite situation [when both blinds are parallel] is referred to as 100% *positive* correlation. 100% positive correlation is customarily assigned a value of +1, while 100% negative correlation is assigned a value of -1.

The crucial part of the experiment comes when we rotate the blinds—the analyzer axes. At 100% positive correlation the angle between the two analyzer axes, or filters, is zero degrees, since they are parallel. But as soon as we rotate one of the filters (it doesn't matter which), *the correlations begin to decrease.* They continue to decrease steadily (the sunglasses darken) as the rotation proceeds until they vanish completely at an angle of 45 degrees. At an angle of 45 degrees the correlations are totally random—there are as many positive as there are negative correlations. This means that *half* the light still gets through. As the rotation of the two filters continues further, less and less light penetrates, until at an angle of 90 degrees [one venetian blind vertical and the other horizontal] no light at all penetrates. The negative or anti-correlation is 100%.

It is interesting that both classical and quantum theory agree on this result. Where they differ, and differ *profoundly*, is the *manner* in which the correlations fall off as the angle between the polarization analyzers, or filters, widens. Classical realism sees the coefficient of correlation changing in one way and quantum theory in another, and the difference—while it may not seem very impressive to some—is absolutely crucial for our view of how the world is put together. If the world is put together along the lines of local realism, as Einstein argued, only a limited number of things are possible. If, on the other hand, the universe functions according to principles that are non-local, a great many more things are possible.

What John Bell's theorem did was to set the limits on the possible in a locally realistic world. In terms of the polarization experiment that we have been discussing, Bell argued that whatever change occurs in the correlations as the angle between the two filters widens ought to be expressible as the outcome of two separate and independent events, namely, as the result of what happens when we rotate filter "A" and as the result of what happens when we rotate filter "B". Since both filters can be rotated independently of one another, without "disturbing" the other in any way, local reality theory would dictate that what happens to the correlations between the photons ought to be the simple sum of what happens first, when filter "A" is rotated, and then second, when filter "B" is rotated. As Menas Kafatos and Robert Nadeau have put it, "If locality holds, and no signal can travel faster than light, turning the right filter can change only the right sequence and turning the left filter can change only the left sequence."[51] One might therefore expect that doubling the angle between the two filters, for example, by rotating each independently in opposite directions, would also double the error rate in the correlations. However, it does nothing of the kind. When one doubles the angle between the two filters from 30 to 60 degrees, this *triples* the error rate. Such an outcome is *impossible* in a locally realistic world. [see Appendix "A"]

Figure (1) on the next page shows just what the differences are in the correlations predicted by quantum theory and those that follow from a simple theory of local realism. The curvilinear path that is traced out by quantum theory indicates 'extra' correlations at every angle except 0, 45, and 90 degrees, where the results of the two theories are the same. There is an exact formula for the quantum correlations, namely cos.[2] (θ), where (θ) is the relative angle between the two filters. There is no unique formula for locally realistic theory, but the diagram shows that the correlations for locally realistic theory are in every instance [except 0, 45, and 90 degrees] significantly *weaker* than those of quantum theory. What this means is that *no locally realistic theory* can produce all of the correlations of quantum theory. Hence, if the correlations predicted by quantum theory really and truly exist, *they must be the result of non-local factors.*

FIGURE 1

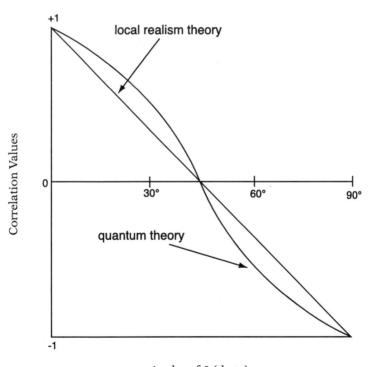

Angles of θ (theta)

What these non-local factors might be remains a mystery. As we have seen, Einstein believed they were illusory. However, laboratory experiments which were done in the years following the publication of Bell's Theorem proved that the universe, at the very least, was a great deal more complex than anyone had thought. "The universe", noted the British biologist J.B.S. Haldane, "is not only queerer than we suppose; it is queerer than we *can* suppose."

Is there a "reasonable" explanation of why the universe should work this way? Perhaps not, but a key to the 'extra' correlations unearthed in these quantum relationships may lie in the notion of quantum wholeness—one of Bohr's favorite phrases. That wholeness, in turn, may reside in the fact that, in the polarization experiment, the relative angle under consideration at any time is always one that is *common to both analyzers.* It is always a *joint* angle of both axes and *cannot* be broken up into separate angles belonging to one analyzer or the other. It is impossible to avoid affecting this joint angle by changing the orientation of just one analyzer, one filter, such as locally realistic theory assumes can be done. That, in my opinion, is why the locality assumption in this instance does not hold.

If the correlations are a joint product of an angle that is necessarily relative to both filters, then the system is indeed a single one, as Bohr maintained. It represents an "unanalyzable whole" in which the measuring instruments, that is, the two analyzers, play a part in the outcome that cannot be divorced from the results obtained. That is, in a nutshell, the essential difference between the quantum view and that of any local realistic theory. The quantum view is that the parts do not have an independent reality of their own, but only exist as elements of an integrated whole in which the parts are mysteriously related to one another through a non-local influence. When one part changes, the others change as well, as does the whole to which they individually and collectively contribute. What one finds difficult to understand, nevertheless, is what possible physical meaning one can attach to the notion of a *relative angle* when the measuring instruments, the filters, are postulated as being situated millions of miles apart. Even in this case the multiple correlations predicted by quantum theory are supposed to exist. It is this notion of superluminal connections across vast spatially separated distances that continues to boggle the mind.

Although the bell seems to have tolled for locality, Bell's Theorem did not, *per se*, prove Bohr right and Einstein wrong about the EPR experiment; that proof came a decade or two later. Bell's Theorem merely provided a *formula* for distinguishing between the views of the two men. When this formula was subsequently put to the test, most convincingly by Alain Aspect in 1982, the 'real' world turned out to be a much more highly correlated quantum place than Einstein gave it any 'right' to be. There clearly *were* "spooky actions at a distance" that were non-local in nature and that Einstein's local realism was at a loss to explain.

On the other hand, precisely *because* such a highly correlated universe exists, the suggestion that these correlations are due to 'chance' or to an 'irreducible lawlessness', as most quantum theorists assume, cannot be correct.

Einstein had expressed his conviction that something other than chance ruled the universe in his famous comment, "God does not play dice". He had always believed that there was a real causal influence at work in the electron's quantum 'jumps', as well as in the process of radioactive decay, and that this causal influence was the same in both. Although he was mistaken, apparently, in his denial of non-locality, he appears to have been correct about causality. Things in the natural world do not happen without 'reason'; there is no free will among electrons. It is hard, in fact, to assign a meaning to total, unmitigated randomness. Bell's Theorem implies that what happens at the quantum level is *not* a matter of pure chance but is the result of a more fundamental, if veiled, determinism. In the words of Henry Stapp:

"Bell's Theorem shows that the macroscopic responses cannot be independent of faraway causes. This problem is neither resolved nor alleviated by saying that the response is determined by 'pure

chance'. Bell's Theorem proves precisely that the
determination of the macroscopic response must be
'non-chance', at least to the extent of allowing some
sort of dependence of this response on the faraway
cause."[52]

So Einstein wins at least a moral victory. If God plays dice,
then we know at least that the dice are 'loaded'. But there may be
more to it than this. David Bohm has speculated that there is an
"implicate order" which is "enfolded" into the universe, and he
has shown in his hypothesis of a *Pilot Wave* and of a *Quantum
Potential* that a non-local realistic theory compatible with all the
statistical predictions of orthodox quantum mechanics is possible.
Bohm's work suggests that non-local correlations need not impose
a strict agnosticism on our pursuit of what is 'real', or, for that
matter, force us to accept Bohr's renunciation of any underlying
reality altogether. Bohm comes down in Einstein's camp, by and
large, on the issue of an objective physical 'reality' that is 'out
there' independent of human measurement or observation.
However, this turns out to be a non-local reality unlike any that
Einstein ever imagined. But before we plunge into this mael-
strom, with all its physical and metaphysical implications, I want
to digress briefly to discuss the nature of the empirical evidence
which breathed life into John Bell's conclusions.

ELEVEN

THE ASPECT
EXPERIMENTS

"The Aspect experiments create great difficulties for local reality...
(they) leave the realist with a lot of explaining to do."
–Jim Baggott

B ell's discovery, because it dealt with theoretical matters
that left unaltered the practical daily routine of most
physicists, did not exactly drop like a bombshell into the
lap of the scientific community. Some physicists, however, saw it
for what it was, namely, a way to finally resolve the long-running
EPR dispute which had been simmering on the back burner of
physics labs for decades. Among the latter were, notably, a number of American physicists, John F. Clauser and Stuart J.
Freedman, who made the first attempts at measuring the *actual*
correlations for pairs of polarized photons I have described, and
four Frenchmen, Alain Aspect, Philippe Grangier, Gérard Roger,
and Jean Dalibard, who made a series of more exacting and
more definitive tests in the early 'eighties, some ten years later.

I shall not go into the technical details of how these experiments were performed, which in any case would be of little
interest to the average reader, except to state that the first experiments—although supportive of the predictions of quantum theory—were inconclusive owing to the existence of a number of

'loopholes'. One of these loopholes, which had to do with the fact that the polarizer orientations were switched too slowly to exclude the possibility of information somehow 'leaking' from one detector to the other, was decisively eliminated in the later, more refined, experiments of Alain Aspect and his associates.

The Aspect experiments had to overcome the possibility of one photon 'knowing' what the other was doing, as the result of some sort of a signal, by switching the orientations of the detectors *while the photons were still in flight.* In order to ensure this result Aspect had to switch the detectors at superluminal speed—thus guaranteeing spatial separability—within the span of about ten nanoseconds [ten billionths of a second], a period of time four times shorter than it would take a signal, traveling at the speed of light, to span the gap between them, a space of only twenty-six feet. This was accomplished by a remarkable acousto-optical switching device, one for each detector, that was activated by passing standing ultrasonic waves through water, thereby altering the refractive index of the water and hence the path of the light passing through it. The end result was equivalent to changing the relative orientations of the two polarization analyzers while the photons were in flight. Any possible communication between the photons regarding the experimental setup would therefore have had to take place at superluminal speed if it were to occur at all.

The Aspect experiments strongly verified the photon correlations predicted by quantum theory, yielding in effect the curvilinear relationship shown in Figure (1). Here is what physicist Jim Baggott has to say about these experiments, which were repeated more than 200 times over a period of several years, each time with increased precision.

> "These results provide almost overwhelming evidence in favor of quantum theory against all classes of locally realistic theories...so where does all this leave local reality? ...We would need to invoke a very grand conspiracy indeed to salvage local

hidden variables from these results... Either we give up reality or we accept that there can be some kind of 'spooky action at a distance', involving communication between distant parts of the world at speeds faster than that of light... Although the independent reality advocated by the realist does not have to be a local reality, it is clear that the experiments described here leave the realist with a lot of explaining to do. An observer changing the orientation of a polarizer *does* affect the behaviour of a distant photon, no matter how distant it is. Whatever the nature of reality, it cannot be as simple as we might have thought at first."[53]

The Aspect experiments do not close all *conceivable* loopholes, but they are as conclusive as any experiment in physics is likely to get. Physicist John Gribben has these observations:

"...The Aspect experiment and its predecessors do indeed make for a very different world view from that of our everyday common sense. They tell us that particles that were once together in an interaction remain in some sense parts of a single system, which responds together to further interactions. Virtually everything we see and touch and feel is made up of collections of particles that have been involved in interactions with other particles right back through time, to the Big Bang in which the universe as we know it came into being. The atoms in my body are made of particles that once jostled in close proximity in the cosmic fireball with particles that are now part of a distant star... Indeed, the particles that make up my body once jostled in close proximity with the particles that now make up your body. We are as much parts of a single system as the two photons flying out of the heart of the Aspect experiment... Theorists such as (Bernard) d'Espagnat and David Bohm argue that we must accept that, literally, everything is connected to everything else, and only a holistic approach to the universe is likely to explain phenomena such as human consciousness."[54]

John Bell, himself, in 1985, added this thought:

"Aspect is a very important experiment, and perhaps it marks the point where one should stop and think for a time, but I certainly hope it is not the end. I think that the probing of what quantum mechanics means must continue, and in fact it will continue, whether we agree or not that it is worth while, because many people are sufficiently fascinated and perturbed by this that it will go on."[55]

And go on it will, because Bell, Aspect, Einstein, Bohr, and other twentieth century pioneers of physics have opened as many new doors on the universe as they may have closed behind them... assuming that any doors are ever *really* closed. That is what is so fascinating about science; it is an infinite voyage of exploration and discovery in which there can never be any 'final' answers.

In the second part of this book I want to take a peek through a number of these doors, because they suggest that the universe is something wholly other than what we have all been taught. The vistas that the new physics exposes have all sorts of metaphysical implications for those willing to stretch their minds to encompass alternatives that may be radically different. A few of these alternatives may be frankly religious in nature, but that ought not to disqualify them, because science—despite the disclaimers of some of its defenders—has always had a religious content. The god of science has always been *Reason*—a belief in the proposition that the universe functions *rationally* and that it is therefore within man's capacity to understand. This is the underlying faith which drives scientists and without which there would be no point to their activities. Unfortunately, it does not necessarily follow that the world can be completely understood by science, because it is apparently so intricately assembled that it may require a faith beyond science if man is ultimately to come to terms with it. Strangely, it is physics itself which is now pointing man in this direction, toward a view of the world and man's place in it which stands traditional science on its head and puts mind—not matter—first. In my opinion the most exciting scientific finding of the last hundred years is neither relativity nor quantum theory *per se*, but the dramatic shift that has taken place in scientific perspectives. Physicists, especially, no longer see their discipline as a closed system in which final 'truth' is just over the horizon, to be discovered by just a bit of extra effort, making man a master of the universe. The doors have been flung wide open to encompass the possibility of new perspectives, including the religious. One physicist who has played an important role in developing some of these new perspectives is David Bohm, a contemporary of Einstein's and a brilliant innovator in his own right. It is to David Bohm's views on physics and metaphysics that I wish to turn next.

PART II

METAPHYSICS

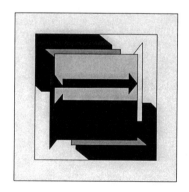

TWELVE

SEEING THINGS WHOLE

"The immeasurable is the primary reality."
–David Bohm

D avid Bohm was one of the most brilliant and innovative theoretical physicists of the twentieth century. He had been brought up on orthodox quantum theory and appeared wholeheartedly in accord with its judgments as laid out by Bohm himself in a book called *Quantum Theory* which he published in 1951. However, he had been heavily influenced by Einstein [later, also, by Krishnamurti], and almost before the ink was dry on his 1951 *oeuvre* he was having second thoughts. Starting in 1952, with the publication of several articles in *Physical Review*, then in 1957 with his new work *Causality and Chance in Modern Physics,* he proceeded to kick over the traces. The effort came to full fruition in 1980, following the development of a realistic quantum theory of his own, with the publication of his *Wholeness and the Implicate Order.* In this landmark work Bohm admitted that he had "never been able to discover any well-founded reasons as to why there exists so high a degree of confidence in the general principles of the current form of the quantum theory."

Nevertheless, Bohm clearly accepted many of those principles, notably the idea of quantum wholeness and the unanalyzability of a quantum system's separate parts, a point of view that Neils Bohr had defended so strongly.

In 1951 Bohm had written:

> "...Quantum theory requires us to give up the idea that the electron, or any other object, has, by itself, any intrinsic properties at all. Instead, each object should be regarded as something containing only incompletely defined potentialities that are developed when the object interacts with an appropriate system... [Quantum theory] contradicts an assumption that has long been implicit in physics...namely, that the universe can be correctly regarded as made up of distinct and separate parts that work together according to exact causal laws to form the whole. In the quantum theory we have seen that none of the properties of these 'parts' can be defined, except in interaction with other parts, and that, moreover, different kinds of interactions bring about the development of different kinds of 'intrinsic' properties of the so-called 'parts'. *It seems necessary, therefore, to give up the idea that the world can correctly be analyzed into distinct parts, and to replace it with the assumption that the world is basically a single, indivisible unit...* "[56] [italics mine]

Subsequently, in 1975, commenting on the concept of non-locality to which Bell's Theorem pointed, Bohm wrote:

> "One is led to a new notion of unbroken wholeness which denies the classical idea of the analyzability of the world into separately and independently existing parts... We have reversed the usual

classical notion that the independent 'elementary' parts of the world are the fundamental reality and that the various systems are merely particular contingent forms and arrangements of these parts. Rather, we say that inseparable quantum interconnectedness of the whole universe is the fundamental reality, and that relatively independently behaving parts are merely particular and contingent forms within this whole."[57]

I think it is difficult to overstate how profound a shift from previous ways of scientific thinking this represents. Before the advent of the quantum era classical physics had always regarded the universe as a collection of separate and independently existing objects. These objects were somehow tied together through a number of fundamental laws, but these laws were local, meaning that their effects fell off with distance, so that the independent action of distant parts of the universe could be practically assumed. This attitude is grounded in everyday experience, in which we all take it for granted that objects exist independently from one another and are only acted upon when they come into proximity. Underlying our approach to the objects we encounter, whether as layman or as scientists, is a tendency to group them into meaningful types and relationships. We look for order, and we discover it in similar differences and different similarities. When scientists think they have discovered a consistent or a repetitive pattern in these relationships, they formulate a behavioral theory connecting them and then proceed to test the theory against its predictions. That is the scientific 'method'. If the predictions hold, the theory becomes accepted as 'correct'—at least until some unexplained anomaly arises that requires the formulation of a new or modified hypothesis. In this way scientists are constantly trying to construct larger and larger 'wholes'. Their ultimate goal is an all-encompassing 'final' theory that will explain *everything*. Scientists, however, are loath to embrace a *discontinuity*, a break in the chain of causality which they can't explain but must simply *accept*. Hence, they tend to assume that any new qualities or attributes of the wholes which they have conjured up somehow *emerge* out of the specific arrangement of their parts. This philosophy is called *emergism* and is especially rampant today in the field of biology.

Alternatively, or perhaps coincidentally, scientists have also followed a philosophy of *reductionism*, in which they start with a concept of the whole and then seek an understanding of why it functions as it does by examining its structure and its behavioral characteristics in the minutest detail. The philosophy of reductionism has been almost universally practiced by scientists until the present day, but it has failed in quantum physics because interactions between quantum entities are not mechanical or classical in any sense. The 'wholes' that are witnessed on the quantum level are simply unexplainable in terms of any simple summation of their parts. Quantum relationships strike at the heart of everything that we have heretofore considered 'rational'. Einstein, as noted, did not believe that non-local effects existed because they were not 'rational'. Such effects, nevertheless, *are* predicted by quantum theory and have now been verified by the empirical evidence—always the court of last resort. But long before this evidence was obtained [by Aspect, et al., as explained in the previous chapter] the view that the universe could be considered as simply a collection of independently existing parts was becoming untenable. Our dilemma is that, while quantum theory has now thoroughly destroyed that notion, it has not given us anything credible to put in its place. What it has given us, instead, is an algorithm and a vacuum, or an infinity of parallel universes, which no one in his right mind could take for 'reality'. The dilemma that quantum theory poses is that we have found no ultimate 'building-blocks'— only a frenetic dance of some 200 'virtual' particles seething and pulsating in the vacuum. When we peer behind the wizard's curtain, we find—nothing. Or, rather, what we find is the so-called "zero-point" energy of the vacuum, potentially limitless, out of which the entire known universe is believed to have been created.

In the quantum world we simply cannot 'add up' the parts to

make any sense of the wholes that we are familiar with, because there aren't any identifiable parts to add up. The universe is not put together that way. It is not a collection of objectively and independently existing parts that are related to one another in any causally unambiguous fashion. As David Bohm has stated, there are no "intrinsic" properties of the separate parts of the universe that we have conceptualized to exist. None of the properties we have defined as attributable to certain 'parts' can be identified as existing except in interaction with other parts. We therefore have no choice but to conclude that the universe is not a fragmented collection of independent objects but that *it is one single organic whole*, in which the parts play an entirely subsidiary role. In David Bohm's conception these subsidiary parts exist only as functioning individual manifestations of the entire organism.

This is a radically different conception of the world than the one by which we seem to come 'naturally', but F. David Peat has come up with a mundane example of it in the vortex of a swiftly flowing river. The vortex has certain characteristics and a definite location in the river, but it is at all times a function of the formative process of the water. It is not a separate entity existing independently, nor is the river a collection of vortices and other areas of calm or turbulence. Another example, perhaps, is a rainbow, which also has structure and a certain relative autonomy, yet cannot be said to have any independent existence of its own. The best example may be our own material bodies, which are composed of cells that are constantly changing, becoming, vanishing, partaking of life, then dying, thereby giving substance and reality to the living organism which is us. The food we eat, the water we drink, the air we breathe are all somehow magically transformed into these living cells. Yet no one would be willing to describe himself as simply a collection of cells. The whole person is obviously more than that, and the cells of which the body is composed do not lead an independent existence of their own. Rather, their existence is a manifestation of the reality of the entire organism.

David Bohm, perhaps more than any other twentieth century physicist, has not only embraced this alternative way of looking at the world but has applied it to his conception of quantum physics. Bohm's is a top-down approach, which has proven enormously insightful in its frank recognition of the existence of higher-dimensional levels of being. Bohm considers such higher-dimensional levels to be the basic reality in physics, out of which all the operative detail flows, rather than the other way 'round. In Bohm's reformulated quantum theory the whole has much greater significance than the parts and, indeed, determines the behavior and properties of the parts. Bohm's is the view of someone who sees the world as a *creation*, in the same sense that an artist views a painting. From the point of view of the artist, the finished painting is primary, the detail secondary. Meaning resides only in the whole, not in the detail. Bohm has structured a theory of the quantum in which the electron is conceived as an entity that is physically 'real' [in contrast to Bohr's abstraction], but Bohm's views of what constitutes this 'reality' have, like the artist's painting, undergone a number of modifications over the years. In *Wholeness and the Implicate Order* Bohm has written:

> "As is now well known...there can be no conclusive proof of the truth or falsity of a general hypothesis which aims to cover the whole of reality...we merely say that man is continually developing new forms of insight, which are clear up to a point and then tend to become unclear...this means that our theories are to be regarded primarily as ways of looking at the world...rather than as 'absolutely true knowledge of how things are'..."

With the reformulation of Schrödinger's wave mechanics Bohm came down firmly in the realist camp, but his realism, as we shall see, is non-local. In Bohm's reformulation of the Schrödinger equation his main concern is with understanding the physics that underlies the mathematical formalism. He is not content to adopt the attitude of most working physicists that they need not bother their heads about 'meaning' so long as they have an algorithm that produces results. He finds such an attitude stultifying and unproductive of further progress in physics. Once again, Bohm:

> "In the quantum theory as it is now constituted there is no consistent notion at all of what the reality may be that underlies the universal constitution and structure of matter...physicists tend to avoid this issue by adopting the attitude that our overall views concerning the nature of reality are of little or no importance... All that counts is supposed to be the development of mathematical equations that permit us to predict and control the behavior of large statistical aggregates of particles..."[58]

In 1987, on the occasion of his retirement, Bohm explained what had brought him to undertake a task that the great mathematician, John von Neumann, had declared "impossible".

> "The whole development started in Princeton around 1950, when I had just finished my book *Quantum Theory*... What I felt to be especially unsatisfactory was the fact that the quantum theory had no place in it for an adequate notion of an independent actuality, i.e. of an actual movement or activity by which one physical state could pass over into another... My main difficulty was that...the theory could only be discussed in terms of the results of an experiment or an observation...a set of *phenomena* not further analyzable or explainable in any terms at all...I felt particularly dissatisfied with the self-contradictory attitude of accepting the independent existence of the cosmos while one was doing relativity and, at the same time, denying it while one was doing the quantum

theory, even though both theories were regarded as fundamental."[59]

Bohm thus decided to see if he could find another approach. He found it in the *pilot wave* notion that had been conceived by the French physicist, Prince Louis Victor Pierre de Broglie, a quarter century before.

In the early 'twenties, while studying for his doctorate, de Broglie had become convinced that the familiar wave/particle duality of light must work both ways, that is, if waves were particles, then particles must also be waves. De Broglie's was a realistic view of what goes on inside the atom in contrast to the probabilistic interpretation that Born had given to the Schrödinger wave function. De Broglie suggested that the electron was a continuous wave field *and* a pointlike localized particle that was somehow "guided" by the field.[60] In de Broglie's conception the field acts as a "pilot wave", directing the motion of the particle, and thereby simulating wave interference, a conception that Schrödinger visualized as a sort of whitecap [Schaumkamm] riding along on the wave crest. Despite the penetrating originality of this view, de Broglie reluctantly gave it up when strong theoretical objections were raised against it, particularly by Wolfgang Pauli, at the 1927 Solvay Conference. As David Bohm was to note later, had de Broglie's conception, rather than Bohr's, become the 'standard' underlying quantum theory, his own reformulation might not have suffered the criticism of some that it seemed "contrived". Bohm naturally rejected this criticism, considering that the widespread acceptance of the Copenhagen Interpretation as 'standard' following de Broglie's failure to press his case was simply a "historical accident."

As Jim Baggott points out in his book *The Meaning of Quantum Theory*, the pilot wave is a hidden variable theory, but the variable that is hidden is not the pilot wave itself [which is revealed in the behavior and properties of the familiar quantum wave function], but the particle *position*. When David Bohm subsequently took up de Broglie's old idea, Bohm's redevelopment represented the wave function as an *objectively real field*. To every real particle in this field Bohm ascribed a precisely defined position *and* a momentum, notwithstanding the fact that in his 1951 book *Quantum Theory* he had taken a different view. Bohm's thinking underwent a number of changes, and he continued to modify his views on what he considered to be the quantum reality throughout his life as his insights deepened. Beginning with his notion of a *Quantum Potential* and an objectively real particle, Bohm later broadened these ideas to include an *implicate* and an *explicate* order in which, in place of objectively real particles, "particle-like behavior results from the convergence of waves at particular points in space. The waves repeatedly spread out and re-converge, producing 'average' particle-like properties corresponding to the constant enfoldment and unfoldment of the wave function. This 'breathing motion' is governed by a super quantum potential related to the wave function of the whole universe."[61] Bohm himself explains: "What we have here is a kind of universal process of constant creation and annihilation determined through the super quantum potential so as to give rise to a world of form and structure in which all manifest features are only relatively constant, recurrent, and stable aspects of this whole."[62]

Bohm's vision is almost metaphysical—in fact, that is precisely how I would describe it. In his last book, with B.J. Hiley, [The Undivided Universe], published just after Bohm's death in 1992, Bohm asks:

> "What is the relationship between the physical and the mental processes? The answer that we propose here is that...both are essentially the same. This means that what we experience as mind, in its movement through various levels of subtlety, will in a natural way ultimately move the body by reaching the level of the quantum potential and of the 'dance' of the particles. There is no unbridgeable gap or barrier between any of these levels...at each stage some kind of *information* is the

bridge...[italics mine] What may be suggested further is that such participation goes on to a greater collective mind, and perhaps ultimately to some yet more comprehensive mind capable of going indefinitely beyond even the human species as a whole...the deeper reality is something beyond either mind or matter...life is eternally enfolded in matter and more deeply in the underlying ground of a generalized holomovement, as is mind and consciousness...the notion of a separate organism is clearly an abstraction, as is also its boundary...underlying all this is unbroken wholeness... (nevertheless) We are not asserting finality for any of the ideas that we propose here...all proposals are points of departure for exploration... We are therefore free, if we so choose, to explore the broader approach to mind and matter, and therefore to the whole of reality, that we have been discussing here."[63]

Whatever the reader may think of these ruminations, he will recognize in them the progressive development of Bohm's thinking. That evolution began with a recognition on Bohm's part that orthodox quantum theory, as Einstein had contended, was "incomplete". The essential difference between Bohm's and Bohr's view, I would say, lies in something called the *Quantum Potential*. The Quantum Potential (Q) is a *new* force that Bohm hypothesized in order to explain wave/particle duality, much as a previous generation had hypothesized the luminiferous ether. Bohm defended himself against the criticism that there was no evidence in favor of a quantum potential by citing physicists' acceptance of the propagation of light and gravity through empty space in the absence of any obvious supporting medium. Bohm writes:

"A steel cable having the diameter of the Earth would not be strong enough to hold the Earth in its orbit around the sun. Yet the gravitational force that holds the Earth in its orbit is transmitted across 93,000,000 miles of space without any trace of a material medium in which these forces might be carried..."

The same, notes Bohm, is true of the propagation of light, yet scientists have not stopped believing in the propagation of light through so-called 'empty' space simply for lack of evidence of a medium.

"Instead, what was done was simply to assume the existence of (electromagnetic) fields without reference to the question of whether or not the ether existed...all that had been significant thus far were the fields themselves. As a result, there arose the notion that the fields are qualitatively new kinds of entities, which we have the same right to postulate as we have to postulate material bodies (such as atoms), provided that such a postulate will help in the explanation of a large range of facts and experimental results... This point of view is now held by a majority of physicists."[64]

Bohm's assumption of a Quantum Potential is no more *ad hoc*, it would appear, than Bohr's assumption of quantum 'jumps' or the ghostly reality of the wave function. It is certainly far less bizarre than the assumption of a multiplicity of universes—and a multiplicity of personal selves—constantly splitting off from one another—an assumption concerning quantum measurement that raises no eyebrows among many physicists. The history of science is replete with various untestable assumptions, the best example being perhaps the Big Bang itself, which cannot be replicated. So Bohm, in my view, is entitled to his Quantum Potential. Its only really novel feature is its assumed constant strength; it does not, like the other fundamental forces of physics, diminish with distance. It is precisely this feature of the Quantum Potential that makes Bohm's new ontology non-local, thus exempting it from the strictures of Bell's Inequality. But, as Aspect has shown, non-locality *is* the new reality, and it says a lot for Bohm's theory that, in the four decades which have passed since it was first formulated, "No sustainable objections against it have ever been made."[65]

In the next chapter I want to take a closer look at this mysterious new force, the Quantum Potential, that Bohm has postulated so that we may possibly understand it better.

THIRTEEN

BOHM'S QUANTUM ONTOLOGY

"There is no reason to suppose that physical theory is
approaching some final truth... We regard all theories
as approximations... There is no final theory."
–*D. Bohm*

I have already indicated why David Bohm was dissatisfied with
orthodox quantum theory. However, when he originally proposed his reformulation, he did it principally to prove that, the
great von Neumann notwithstanding, there *was* a realistic quantum alternative. Bohm resurrected the notion of hidden variables
in order to liberate contemporary physics from the dead hand of
stagnation which it seemed to have reached following the inconclusive Bohr-Einstein debates. In the introduction to his last book,
The Undivided Universe, published jointly in 1992 with B.J. Hiley,
Bohm reiterates the reasons why what he describes as an "ontological interpretation" is called for. These are:

1. Quantum theory's inability to "describe individual quantum processes without bringing in unsatisfactory
   assumptions, such as the collapse of the wave function."

2. The "well-known non-locality that has been brought out by
   Bell in connection with the EPR experiment."

3. The "mysterious wave-particle duality."

4. "Above all, the inability to give a clear notion of what the reality of a quantum system could be."

> "All that is clear about the quantum theory is that it contains an algorithm for computing the probabilities of experimental results. But it gives no physical account of individual quantum processes. Indeed, without the measuring instruments in which the predicted results appear, the equations of the quantum theory would be just pure mathematics that would have no physical meaning at all. And thus quantum theory merely gives us...knowledge of how our instruments will function...quantum theory can say little or nothing about reality itself."[66]

This had been, in essence, also Einstein's position, but Einstein was opposed to the idea of non-local action and so, following EPR, had little further to say about the matter. Bohm, however, who was considerably Einstein's junior, was sufficiently stimulated by the latter's views that he determined to reopen the question that von Neumann's intimidating reputation seemingly had foreclosed.

In Bohm's preliminary reformulation of the quantum theory the notion of a *Quantum Potential* plays a central role. Yet exactly what this concept represents is still something of a mystery. The answer which Bohm gives is that the Quantum Potential represents *active information*, but what is the meaning of this expression? "The basic idea of active information", Bohm has indicated, "is that a form having very little energy enters into and directs a much greater energy."[67] Bohm gives the example of an ocean liner, which is propelled through the sea by its own power but is nevertheless subtly guided, perhaps by radar, to avoid obstacles in its path. He has extended this analogy to the image of a radio receiver, where the power of the receiver may be provided by a battery but where its audible output is entirely dependent on the form of the incoming radio wave. An analogy that I find compelling is to the codified information of a DNA strand, where the *specified complexity* of its nucleotides is what renders the DNA sequence meaningful.[68] Bohm explains that the Quantum Potential is entirely dependent on the *mathematical form* of the quantum field, which may be subject to extremely rapid random oscillations at some deeper sub-quantum level "in much the same way that the fluctuations in the Brownian motion of a microscopic liquid come from a deeper atomic level."[69] The raw energy of the electron itself, Bohm speculates, may originate in the vast, unexplored, sub-quantum realm that is readily conceivable between the shortest distances now measurable in physics [10^{-16}cms] and the shortest distances in which our current notions of space-time structure probably have meaning [10^{-33}cms]. This range of scale, Bohm notes, "is comparable to that which exists between our own size and that of the elementary particle."[70] The energy of this undefined sub-quantum structure, in turn, is possibly attributable to the fluctuations of the vacuum that is thought to be a feature of this structure and whose total "zero-point" energy is beyond calculation. All of this, of course, is highly speculative (although no more so than the notion of a quantum 'jump'), but it is precisely this kind of imaginative yet informed thinking that has always preceded the greatest advances in physics. In Bohm's view the electron, or any other elementary particle, has a rich and complex inner structure, and it is this which enables it to respond so sensitively to the active information provided by the field and its quantum potential. In Bohm's ontology the field is a causally determined reality, but it is the mathematical *form* of the field alone, and not its amplitude, which guides the energy of the self-movement of the particle. Thus, when the form of the field is altered, for example, when it passes through the double slits, the entire quantum potential changes, instantly, in a non-local manner. Readers may recall the polarization experiment described in connection with Bell's Theorem. When either polarizing filter was reoriented, this immediately changed the relative angle of *both* filters, thereby radically altering the polarization correlations. Bohm's interpretation would be that the reorientation instantly changes the wave function of the *whole* system, and hence also its quantum potential, thus redistributing its possibilities for actualization.

If we adopt Bohm's view of the existence of a Quantum Potential subject to instantaneous change, then the issue of non-locality can be detached from the notion that it is necessary to send a *signal* from one location to another in order to affect a distant quantum state. It was the notion of *signaling* between space-like separated systems that had so distressed Einstein. The sending of a superluminal signal carrying some sort of information is clearly incompatible with relativity. But, as Bohm points out, the whole notion of what constitutes a 'signal' becomes moot in the face of a common *wholeness*, because a signal presupposes separation and independence of parts. That is why, as John Polkinghorne correctly surmises, there is no necessary contradiction between quantum wholeness and Einsteinian relativity, and it is why analogies to superluminal signaling are misleading. The Quantum Potential represents the total environment in which quantum events take place. When the Quantum Potential changes, it is like shifting, instantaneously, the stage scenery in a play. When the scenery changes, the possibilities for action *on the entire stage* are altered, without the need for any cues between the players. To broaden the analogy, the lines spoken by the actors do not determine the play; rather, the play determines the actors' lines. The central idea is that it is not the parts which determine the whole, but the whole which determines the parts. In the polarization experiment involving photons the changing relative angle between the two analyzers cannot be broken down into separate angles that affect only what happens at one location, because the angle is necessarily common to *both* locations. In the same way, the Quantum Potential is common to what happens *everywhere* in the field, so that, when it changes, its strength being constant, this immediately changes all possibilities *everywhere*. It is thus not a question of a signal being sent from point to point to effect a change, but of a common *wholeness* that is all-pervasive.

One way for the reader to visualize this is via Karl Popper's pinboard. Popper, an Einstein realist and an influential philosopher of science, came up with the notion of a pinboard in reflecting upon Bohm's Quantum Potential. The pinboard image of a marble entering an inclined plane and then watching it descend through the maze of pins, in zig-zag fashion, toward an exit near the bottom, will be familiar to everyone. Now, if the pins are identical, and no other force acts upon the marble, its progress toward the exit will be determined solely by the immediate physical factors involved [board inclination, pin arrangement, and the marble itself]. Popper has called this joint determinism of the whole system its *propensity* to yield a certain result. This propensity, though not each outcome, will remain constant until there is some change in the whole arrangement. Popper's *propensity*, notes Jim Baggott, may be likened to Bohm's *Quantum Potential*, "Q". The slightest change in the system's propensity alters its probabilities of delivering a given result, and it does so instantly and across the board.

Still another image may appeal to those readers familiar with the ancient game of chess. Chess is played on a board with 64 squares of alternating color, with the opposing black and white pieces—the chessmen—lined up along either end of the board. The starting lineup of each player's pieces is the mirror image of the other's. Note that the *potential for action* is not quite the same for both players as the game begins, since white has the advantage of the first move and black must adapt his strategy accordingly. Moreover, the potential for action changes, for both players, constantly throughout the game, depending on what moves are made. When the situation on the board changes, this instantly affects the potential future development of the game for both participants. The outcome of the game cannot be viewed, as in golf, as a simple summation of the independent actions of the two opponents. In chess the potential for action changes instantly, across the board, whenever one of them makes a move. No signaling of any kind, superluminal or otherwise, is involved.

What happens in chess has some similarity, I think, to Bohm's Quantum Potential, as an alteration of the situation anywhere affects the possibilities available to the electron during a quantum measurement. In the double slit experiment the path that an electron may take as it moves toward the monitoring screen is governed, in Bohm's conception, by a *Quantum Potential* which is instantly affected by any change in the slit arrangement, measuring instruments included. When one of the slits is closed, the possibilities available to the electron during a quantum measurement are instantly changed, and the electron alters its behavior accordingly. The changed situation affects the electron as a non-local event, as reflected in a modification of the entire potential within which it operates, as described by "Q". The closing of one of the holes, or slits, affects the *form* of the wave function which, according to Bohm, guides the energy of the self-movement of the particle. The change in the potential for the quantum system, as in chess, is not the result of an act of communication but is entirely the result of a change of *state*. This change of state for the quantum system, as in chess, is all-pervasive, immediate, and non-local.

Lest it be thought that, In Bohm's conception, "Q" is not a quantifiably real force, let it be noted that its value is precisely specifiable mathematically and readily calculable and diagramable by the computer. Figures (2) and (3) following show illustrative computer simulations of the Quantum Potential as well as particle trajectories in the double slit experiment made famous by Thomas Young. Here is what F. David Peat, author of *Einstein's Moon*, has to say about these simulations:

> "Notice that the various paths have a periodically bunched character as they near the screen. Over many experiments, the electrons tend to hit the screen in this periodic bunched manner so as to *give the appearance of an interference pattern* [italics mine]. In Bohm's view, the electron does not have a wave nature; rather, the particular proper-

ties of the quantum potential simulate the appearance of wave interference."[71]

FIGURE 2: COMPUTER SIMULATION OF QUANTUM POTENTIAL

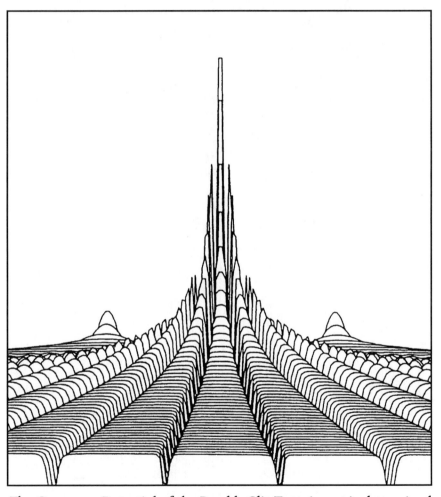

The Quantum Potential of the Double-Slit Experiment is determined by the unique arrangement of the combined apparatus.

FIGURE 3: TRAJECTORIES FOR TWO GAUSSIAN SLIT SYSTEMS

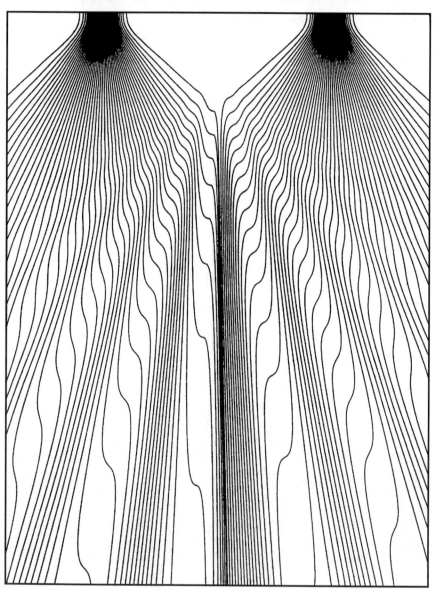

A computer simulation of the trajectories that might be followed by an electron in the Double-Slit Experiment. The pattern produced is one which remarkably simulates one of wave interference.

In the two-slit experiment where the Quantum Potential is altered as it passes through the double slits [Figure 3], the particle trajectories produced by "Q" show a pattern of light and dark fringes that closely resemble those known to result from wave interference. When one of the slits is closed, this pattern instantly changes, because the Quantum Potential instantly changes the wave function. In Bohm's theory, changing the measuring device, which in the polarization experiment might mean re-orienting one or both of the filters, instantly changes the mathematical form of the wave function and therefore also the Quantum Potential, since it is the latter which connects every part of the field into one inseparable whole. Bohm is at pains to make this point:

> "We therefore emphasize that the quantum field is not pushing or pulling the particle mechanically, any more than the radio wave is pushing or pulling the ship that it guides."[72]

What the field is doing, Bohm says, is supplying *active information,* much as a road map supplies information on the territory through which the motorist travels. The particle somehow *responds* to this information in a pre-determined manner, and therein lies the mystery. *Why* the particle responds as it does is no more explainable, ultimately, than is the response of the human cell to the genetic code which supplies *it* with vital information. Physical theories can tell us only the 'hows', not the 'whys', of phenomena, and Bohm's theory is no different in this respect than any other.

The Quantum Potential, if it is real, probably has its origin in a curious property of a quantum system known as *phase entanglement.* Schrödinger considered phase entanglement to be *the* characteristic trait of quantum theory. In the orthodox interpretation of quantum theory the wave function for a two-particle quantum system does not separate as the particles themselves move apart in space-time. As Jim Baggott notes: "Instead of dissolving into completely separate wave functions, one associated with each particle, the wave function is 'stretched out' and, when a measurement is made, collapses instantaneously despite the fact that it may be stretched-out over a large distance."[73] The phases of the two systems somehow remain 'entangled' with one another, though the systems themselves may be millions of miles apart. This supposed 'entanglement' is written into the mathematics of the theory and is what accounts for the non-local aspect of a quantum measurement. The paradox is that, while Bohr and his followers were willing to accord reality status to the phenomena measured by their laboratory instruments, in effect to their point-er readings, they were not willing to accord a counterpart physical reality to the phase entanglement of their equations. All references to physical counterparts as having any fundamental reality in the quantum theory were anathema to the Copenhagen group.

In Bohm's reformulation of quantum theory, on the other hand, the concept of phase entanglement *is* accorded physical reality status, notwithstanding the fact that, as in the orthodox theory, quantum interactions for many-body systems in Bohm's reformulation also take place in what is known as *configuration space*, a multi-dimensional realm that has no counterpart in the universe of our ken. Bohm is willing to accord reality status to this multi-dimensional space because he regards the energy and momentum of the quantum field as being guided by a common, non-physical "pool of information" which depends in a non-local way on the whole wave function, that is, on the system's quantum state. Bohm explains:

> "The fact that the wave function is in configura-
> tion space clearly prevents us from regarding the
> quantum field as one that carries energy and
> momentum"... [in some mechanical way], and
> additionally "...leads us to consider the interpreta-
> tion of this field as *active information*. The multi-
> dimensional nature of this field need not then be
> so mysterious, since information can be organized
> into as many sets of information as may be need-

ed." "We emphasize again", Bohm continues, "...that the notion of active information corresponds to a tremendous range of common experience. We have generally devalued this sort of experience as far as physics is concerned and have assumed that physical laws should contain only mechanical concepts, such as position, momentum, force, etc.... What we are pointing out here is that if we suitably extend the kind of concepts we are willing to admit into physics (e.g. to include active information) then we can gain a much better intuitive apprehension of (quantum) theory."[74]

Bohm is saying that quantum mechanics, viewed in this light, need not remain simply a mathematical algorithm but can become a realistically intelligible theory; The introduction into physics of the concept of the Quantum Potential as a real force informing and subtly guiding the motion of matter in a non-local way at the quantum level is Bohm's unique contribution, I feel, toward a resolution of some of the conceptual and interpretive difficulties that have plagued the quantum theory from its inception. Whether we agree with Bohm in all respects or not, it ought to be admitted that *active information*, as Bohm uses the term, cannot be denied reality status simply on the grounds that it is not mechanical. The evidence that ours is not primarily a mechanical universe is overwhelming. The new evidence [Aspect, et al] that there are non-local, as well as local forces at work, which has long been recognized in the mathematics of quantum theory, is sufficient, in my opinion, to justify the acceptance of a multidimensional reality as underlying Bohm's new concept of the Quantum Potential.

In Bohm's reformulated theory the quantum measurement problem does not arise, because Bohm *starts* from the assumption that a quantum system involves real particles whose trajectories are deterministic and not just superpositions of probable states. There is thus, as Bohm is at pains to emphasize, *no collapse of the wave function in his theory,* although he frankly admits that "everything happens as if the wave function had collapsed... There is no actual collapse; there is merely a process in which the information represented by the unoccupied packets (which Bohm calls 'channels')...effectively loses all potential for activity."[75] Menas Kafatos and Robert Nadeau have commented that Bohm's model does not explain what it is that forces the choice among 'channels'. In Bohm's view which channel is activated, that is, which potentiality is realized, "depends on the observing apparatus as well as on the observed system." Bohm elucidates:

> "A helpful analogy may be obtained by considering a seed, which is evidently not an actual plant, but which determines potentialities for realizing various possible forms of the plant, according to conditions of soil, rain, wind, sunlight, etc., ...The different possible orientations of the (measuring) apparatus correspond...to different environments of the seed, which in turn lead to different forms of the plant. In the case of particles, we can see how changing the orientation of the apparatus changes the quantum potential and how this, in turn, changes the possible states in which the system can be actualized... What all this means...is that quantum properties cannot be said to belong to the observed system alone; ...Such properties have no meaning apart from the total context which is relevant in any particular situation. In this case, this includes the overall experimental arrangement, so that we can say that measurement is context-dependent. The above is indeed a consequence of the fact that quantum processes are irreducibly participatory... The interactions... which depend on the quantum potential can introduce large non-local connections between all the constituents of the total system... This is as if the

basic law of interaction of all the parts were changing in the process in which the observed system and the observing apparatus come into contact. The result is, therefore, in effect, a transformation of the very nature of the system as a whole and of all its constituents. In the quantum case the participation is of a deeper and more fundamental nature than it is classically. Indeed, in classical physics, no matter how much the observed particle is disturbed fundamentally, its basic laws of interaction remain the same...the basic properties...are intrinsic, no matter how strong the interaction may be. But in the quantum theory, such properties can...have meaning only in the total relevant context."[76]

These are not easy concepts to grasp. In comparing his Quantum Potential to the notion of *active information* Bohm notes that:

"...Nothing is more common in ordinary experience than for information to lose its potential for activity. If we accept that the particle is what responds to information at the quantum mechanical level, it is clear that there is no serious problem with the empty wave packets. The essential point is that information is immensely more subtle and less substantial than the systems on which it acts... In a quantum measurement...there is the linear combination of wave functions [between object and measuring instrument]...through this period the two systems are 'guided' by a common pool of information implying a quantum potential that connects them in a non-local way... After the interaction is over...(an interaction in which)...the apparatus and the observed system have *participated*...and have deeply affected each other...we are left with a situation in which the states of the two are correlated, in accordance with the channel that the particles have actually entered... We emphasize again that we do not assume the collapse of the wave function. The particle enters one channel and is only affected by the active information in that channel... There is no paradox in this conclusion...we avoid a paradox (of the conventional interpretation) by *giving up the assumption that the wave function is a complete description of reality* [italics mine]...which is what makes the further assumption of collapse necessary. By introducing the particle's position as *essential for a more complete description* [my emphasis], we turn what was a paradoxical situation into one that is quite simple and straightforward."[77]

"Simple and straightforward", perhaps, to Bohm, but hardly to the average nonscientist. I have nevertheless thought it necessary to dwell at length on the quantum measurement problem because it is at the root of the difficulties of quantum interpretation and I wanted to impress upon you how Bohm has dealt with and circumvented it. Although not everyone will feel comfortable with Bohm's quantum ontology, Bohm has at least done what he set out to do, namely, to come up with an alternative to quantum theory which is based upon the assumption that there is a 'real world out there' behind all the mathematics which has a plausible interpretation. Moreover, he has done it in a way that none of his critics have been able to refute.

But what of indeterminacy, which is so integral a part of the mathematics? What of Heisenberg's Uncertainty Principle? How does this important centerpiece of quantum mechanics fare in Bohm's ontology?

In *Causality and Chance in Modern Physics* Bohm writes as follows:

"...The indeterminacy principle necessitates a renunciation of causality only if we assume that this principle has an absolute and final validity...in every domain that will ever be investigated in physics. On the other hand, if we assume that this principle applies only as a good approximation and only in some limited domain...then room is left open for new kinds of causal laws to apply in new domains... As we shall see, there is good reason to assume the existence of a sub-quantum mechanical level that is more fundamental than that at which the present quantum theory holds... The indeterminacy principle would then apply in the quantum level, and would have no relevance at all at lower levels... The treatment of the indeterminacy principle as absolute and final can then be criticized as constituting an arbitrary restriction on scientific theories, since it does not follow from the quantum theory as such, but rather from the assumption of the unlimited validity of certain of its features, an assumption that can in no way ever be subjected to experimental proof."[78]

I do not know what Heisenberg's *riposte* to these remarks of Bohm's was, but we may guess his reaction. Heisenberg, a confirmed 'Copenhagenist', was convinced that the "more fundamental reality" to which Bohm alluded simply did not exist.

As I have stressed before, and as Bohm is careful to point out, the notion of a *common wholeness* is perhaps *the* most important idea in his ontology, even more important than the notion of the Quantum Potential itself. With respect to this concept of a fundamental and universal wholeness both Bohm and Bohr are of the same mind. But Bohr was never willing to go beyond the mathematics of the quantum theory to envision a physical reality to which its equations corresponded, thus severely limiting his horizon, and the same was true of his followers. Bohr—and

Heisenberg—were concerned only with what they termed "observables", that is, attributes of physical systems which registered on
some kind of measuring instrument. What is ironic about this is
that these so-called "observables" could never be known *directly*.
The only knowledge it was possible to have of them was as pointer
readings on a piece of laboratory apparatus, scintillation flashes
on a phosphorescent screen, or clicks of a Geiger counter—and
then only when an actual measurement took place. At all other
times it was Bohr's view that to speculate about any fundamental
'reality' underlying the measured phenomena was "meaningless".
Only the equations were "real".

Bohm comments on this peculiar attitude to mathematics. He
notes that, until the present century, physical concepts were, for
the most part, considered as primary, while mathematical equations were regarded as providing a more precise way of talking
about these concepts. But,

> "The view has become common among most mod-
> ern theoretical physicists...that the equations are
> their most immediate contact with nature, the
> experiments only confirming or refuting the cor-
> rectness of this contact... So, without an equation,
> there is really nothing to talk about...the insistence
> that one is not to be allowed to conceive of what is
> happening at [the quantum] level means that one
> is restricted to making blind mathematical manip-
> ulations with the hope that, somehow, one of
> these manipulations will lead to a new and correct
> theory..."[79]

Bohm makes it clear that he does not share this modern
view—that it is too limiting—and that much is to be learned by
using physical concepts as a guide for the development of new
equations. In *The Undivided Universe* he writes:

"We have a rather different attitude to the mathematics... [physical concepts and mathematics] should complement each other... Our view is that nature in its totality is unlimited, not merely quantitatively, but also qualitatively in its depth and subtlety of laws and processes...there is no way to prove that any particular aspect of our knowledge is absolutely correct... Ultimately everything plays both the role of appearance and of essence...the ultimate reality is unlimited and unknown...no matter how far we go we are basically involved in perception. Our theories are not primarily forms of knowledge about the world...rather, they are forms of insight that arise in our attempts to obtain a perception of a deeper nature of reality as a whole. As such we do not expect their development ever to come to an end, any more than we would look forward to a final sense perception."[80]

The profundity of Bohm's thinking is evident in these few quotations. Bohm never suffered the delusion that he had latched on to some kind of final truth. His development of the idea of a quantum force or pilot wave in association with the electron underwent several transformations, culminating in his concept of a Super Quantum Potential and an "enfolded" or "implicate" order. These notions are frankly metaphysical, but I think they deserve to be taken seriously because Bohm was, if anything, a serious thinker. Bohm was always conscious of the fact that, in his pursuit of truth through physics, he had been handed a set of keys that opened only a limited number of doors, and that there was an infinity of such doors to be opened. That is why I think you will find, with me, that Bohm's explorations into what he calls the "enfolded" or "implicate" order are so valuable. For these speculations, if you will, are not just the fantasies of some starry-eyed mystic, but the perceptions of one who has devoted his life to understanding the physical world and who has earned the accolades of his peers as one of the most creative thinkers in his field. Follow me, then, in the next chapter as we explore for ourselves some of what Bohm has discovered and share with me in the excitement of these revelations.

FOURTEEN

THE IMPLICATE ORDER

*"The implicate order...(is) a process of enfoldment
and unfoldment in a higher-dimensional space...
which is effectively infinite."*
–D. Bohm

Closely related to David Bohm's conception of quantum wholeness is his notion of 'order'. Now, order, I submit to you, is something that resides in nature; it is not merely a construct of the mind. The dictionary defines order as "methodical or harmonious arrangement". Everywhere we look in nature we see examples of such methodical or harmonious arrangement. We see it in the symmetry of crystals, in the intricate patterns of snowflakes and flowers, in the hive of the bee and the nests of animals, in the regularity of the seasons, and in the entire adaptive behavior of each species of animal to its environment. The irrepressible tendency of nature to express itself in repetitive patterns of increasing complexity, rather than simply as a chaos, is overwhelming evidence that there exist fundamental laws of form and order to which all nature adheres. Even chaos, it turns out, is productive of complex and beautiful patterns of order as seen in the phenomenon of *strange attractors*. These fundamental laws of form and order extend far beyond the simple Darwinist principle of natural selection. They constitute an aspect of universal experience that has hardly yet been addressed by science.

That may be, in part, because they are in principle *integrative processes*—creative processes—whereas science has largely been concerned with *reductionism*. David Bohm is one of the very few theoretical physicists, to my knowledge, who has thought deeply about the notion of order and wholeness. His landmark work, *Wholeness and the Implicate Order,* published in 1980, is not only highly original in its approach to notions of form and order but brings to the subject the knowledge and experience of someone who is also a first-rate physicist.

The perception of order, David Bohm has suggested, is the recognition of similar differences and of different similarities. Such recognition is therefore *ipso facto* the manifestation of some degree of intelligence, whether one thinks of intelligence as symptomatic of conscious thought or as a chemical reaction that has somehow been encoded into the genes. All creatures, from the highest to the lowest, organize their world into a rational, or at least a recognizable, pattern. They *must* do this if they are to be able to adapt to their environment and to survive in the struggle for existence. On the lowest levels of life this effort may be sub-conscious, or even chemical, as I have suggested. On the highest levels of life the proclivity to organize is a clearly conscious force that underlies man's science and, indeed, all of his civilization. On the human level we find that notions of order are almost infinitely varied and that they are as much imposed on the environment through man's preconceptions as they are derived from it as the consequence of natural law. Scientists regard it as an article of faith that there really *is* an underlying order to physical phenomena, or else there could be no inter-subjective agreement among them on the postulates and conclusions of science. For Einstein this was one of the most fundamental questions that could be asked. "What I'm really interested in," said Einstein, "is whether God could have made the world in a different way; that is, whether the necessity of logical simplicity leaves any freedom at all."[81] It was also a deep question for David Bohm. In his *Wholeness and the Implicate Order* Bohm gave free rein to those speculations, posing the question of whether physicists' traditional way of representing order, namely, by a Cartesian grid of space-time coordinates, was the only possible or even the most effective way.

David Bohm did not think so. He had become interested, during the early 'sixties, in fundamental physical notions of order and happened to see a televised science program in which an ink drop was injected into a cylinder of glycerin, then spread out and reconstituted essentially as it had been before. This struck Bohm as very relevant to the question of order, "since when the ink drop was spread out it still had a hidden (i.e. non-manifest) order that was revealed when it was reconstituted."[82] The ink drop was somehow clearly "enfolded" in the glycerin—we would say diffused— and then "unfolded" again, or made explicit, in a manner that fascinated him.

The device that Bohm saw consisted of two concentric glass cylinders, one within the other, with a viscous fluid (glycerin) filling the space between. A droplet of insoluble ink was placed into the fluid and the inner cylinder turned, so that the droplet was drawn out into a fine thread that eventually became invisible as the inner cylinder continued to be rotated. Nevertheless, when the rotation was reversed, the thread again became visible and the entire ink drop was reconstituted in full. Bohm notes:

> "When the ink droplet is drawn out, one is able to see no visible order in the fluid. Yet, evidently, there must be some order there, since an arbitrary distribution of ink particles would not come back to a droplet. One can say that in some sense the ink droplet has been enfolded into the glycerin, from which it unfolds when the movement of the glycerin is reversed... This device gives us an illustrative example of the implicate order."

The same notion of an implicate or enfolded order, Bohm notes, is contained in a hologram. A hologram differs from an ordinary lens in that each region of the hologram contains within itself an image of the whole object, whereas an ordinary lens renders an approximate point to point correspondence of object and image. The hologram does not closely resemble the object at all, but an image may be seen in it when it is suitably illuminated. It does not seem to have any order, and yet there must be something that determines the order of points that appear in the image when illuminated. Bohm was impressed by the similarity of the hologram and the ink drop, in that what they both had in common was an order that was somehow "enfolded" into them.

Now, the notion of "enfoldment" and "unfoldment" is not particularly hard to grasp, but Bohm has attributed to it a certain physical significance that is almost mystical. In commenting on the dichotomy between relativity and quantum theory he notes that, while both theories share a notion of unbroken wholeness, "the basic orders implied in relativity theory and in quantum theory are qualitatively in complete contradiction. Thus, relativity theory requires strict continuity, strict causality, and strict locality in the order of movement of particles and fields... (while) in essence quantum mechanics implies the opposite..."[84] In relativity theory the point-event in space-time is the basic concept, and this is defined in terms of a Cartesian space-time grid. The point-event is thus distinct and separate from all other point-events. This is why many cosmologists prefer the *Many Worlds* interpretation of quantum theory to the *Copenhagen* interpretation; it permits them to retain the idea of separate and distinct point-events in their study of the cosmos.

In quantum theory, on the other hand, "the idea of separate point-events clearly has no place", says Bohm. In the standard version separate and distinct point-events that can be located along a Cartesian grid are accorded no real existence at all. The only 'reality' is an algorithm which permits the *probability* of such point-events to be determined when a measurement is made but to which no physical meaning can be attached. In Bohm's reformulation of quantum theory we can at least visualize a physical reality, although it is not a reality of separate and distinct point-events in conventional space-time. Rather, the system is regarded as an unanalyzable whole in which the quality of "active information" represented by the Quantum Potential provides a non-local connection with distant objects, a connection that obliges us to look at the whole as a single combined system. Hence, our notions of order, which have been conditioned by the classical concept of a Cartesian grid, obviously need revamping in a way that will encompass the wholeness implied by both relativity and quantum theory in a new concept that has the possibility of going beyond both.

It is to this problem that Bohm's development of the concept of the existence of an "implicate" or "enfolded" order is addressed. Bohm proceeds to address it as follows:

> "Basically, the implicate order has to be considered as a process of enfoldment and unfoldment in a higher-dimensional space...the implicate order is a multi-dimensional reality... In principle, this reality is one unbroken whole, including the entire universe, with all its 'fields' and 'particles'. Thus we have to say that the *holomovement* enfolds and unfolds in a multi-dimensional order, the dimensionality of which is effectively infinite. However (from this order) relatively independent sub-totalities can generally be abstracted, which may be regarded as autonomous... It is being suggested here that what we perceive through our senses as empty space is actually the plenum, which is the ground for the existence of everything, including ourselves. The things that appear to our senses are derivative forms, and their true meaning can be seen only when we consider the plenum, in which they are generated and sustained, and into which they must ultimately vanish."[86]

The *plenum*, Bohm explains, actually forms a vast sea of energy, ultimately stemming from the *zero-point energy* of the vacuum, which is literally incalculable. What we call matter is, in Bohm's view, just an "excitation", a "little ripple", on this vast sea of energy. Bohm compares this "little ripple" to the sudden conjunction of myriads of small waves that occasionally come together in the middle of the ocean, forming one large wave that seems to appear as if out of nowhere. He writes:

> "Perhaps something like this could happen in the immense ocean of cosmic energy, creating a sudden wave pulse, from which our 'universe' would be born... It must be remembered that even this vast sea of cosmic energy takes into account only what happens on a scale larger than the critical length of 10^{-33} cms (which)...is only a certain kind of limit on the applicability of ordinary notions of space and time... To suppose that there is nothing at all beyond this limit would indeed be quite arbitrary. Rather, it is very probable that beyond it lies a further domain, or set of domains, of the nature of which we have as yet little or no idea."[87]

Far be it from me to criticize these speculations as 'unscientific' or as 'unreasonable', because Bohm was much too competent a physicist to indulge in science fiction. Certainly, they are no more unreasonable than some of the assumptions that underlie currently accepted physical theories, such as *Many Worlds*, for example, or even quantum theory with its weird element of "ghost" fields and non-locality. What Bohm's speculations underline, so far as I am concerned, is how far we have drifted, in the short space of 100 years, from the comfortable, classical type universe that scientists believed in at the start of the twentieth century to the mind-boggling concepts of today. The observation cannot have escaped the reader that the study of physics is as wide open today as it appeared closed to most scientists approximately a century ago.

Another sentiment that comes through very strongly in all this is how the horizons of science constantly recede from one generation to another as physicists build new theories, just as the real horizon of man's experience keeps fading into the distance. I share with Bohm the conviction that there literally are no limits to this recession, an idea that many scientists, including Einstein, have echoed. As David Finkelstein, a professor of physics at Georgia Tech has put it, "If there is no final answer, it is simply that there is no final question." Bohm's conception of an *implicate order* is in no sense 'final', as Bohm would be the first to admit, but it has proven immensely illuminating, in my judgment. In the following chapter we are going to explore some of the implications of the enormous changes in scientific knowledge and in scientific perspective that have occurred in the last hundred years and what we may learn from them.

FIFTEEN

A REALITY BEYOND PHYSICS

"Science cannot solve the ultimate mystery of nature...
because, in the last analysis, we ourselves are part
of the mystery we are trying to solve."
–Max Planck

The revolution that has shaken physics during the last hundred years is quite remarkable in its scope and depth, but equally remarkable is the shift in scientific and philosophical perspective which has accompanied it. This shift in perspective, from that of a closed, mechanical, and deterministic universe about which leading scientists thought almost everything had been learned, to an open, non-local, holistic universe where ultimate truth is up for grabs, has brought with it a great deal of confusion and uncertainty, but it also has proven intellectually rewarding. We now know—if we didn't know it before—that science has no monopoly on truth and that science is often heavily dependent on frankly speculative assumptions, being in this respect no different from other belief systems. All of science is based on the belief (faith) that the world is rational. It was his faith in a rational universe that caused Einstein to declare that he didn't believe that God played dice. Bohr's reply to this, "But still, it cannot be for us to tell God how he is to run the world", reflects a different kind of faith, but one that is still founded on a belief in order. Bohm's vision of an "implicate order", operating behind the scenes, so-to-speak, yet enfolding everything, also reveals a profound faith that the universe is not a chaos, but has a hidden meaning. Not many scientists, in fact, when they are pressed, are willing to place a very heavy bet on atheism. Steven Weinberg's remark that "The more the universe seems comprehensible, the more it also seems pointless" has, as Weinberg is frank to admit, "drawn more negative comments than...anything else I've ever written."[88] Most scientists today, I gather, are at least willing to concede that there is still a deep mystery at the heart of physics, which the best minds have not been able to unravel, though the cockiest among them continue to insist that an ultimate solution is only a matter of time. The most profound thinkers, to whom both Bohm and Einstein belong, do not expect this process of discovery to come to an end; they do not expect to find a 'theory of everything' at the end of the rainbow. Rather, as David Bohm writes in *The Undivided Universe*, "Nature in its totality is unlimited, not only quantitatively, but also qualitatively in its depth and subtlety of laws and processes." Or, as Gottfried Leibnitz put it more than three centuries ago, "You will find that, when you are admitted to the heart of nature, the farther you go the greater will be your delights, because you will be only at the beginning of a chain that goes on to infinity."[89]

Steven Weinberg, on the other hand, still dreams of a 'final theory'—the title of his latest book. Weinberg poses, then answers, the question: "Will we find an interested God in the final laws of nature?" in the negative. The whole idea is "premature", if not "absurd", thinks Weinberg, "not only because we do not yet know the final laws but much more because it is difficult to imagine being in the possession of ultimate principles that do not need any explanation in terms of deeper principles."[90] Weinberg seems to be conceding here that there may be an infinity of such deeper principles which would make any final, all-inclusive 'Theory of Everything' impossible.

In fact, the impossibility of ever arriving at such a final theory, at least in a mathematical sense, had already been demonstrated more than fifty years earlier by the brilliant Austrian mathematician, Kurt Gödel. Gödel formulated in 1931 what is now known as the *Incompleteness Theorem*, which in a nutshell, as Stanley Jaki notes, "states the futility of chasing one's own intellectual tail."[91] More precisely, the Incompleteness Theorem states that, in any formal non-trivial mathematical system, there must be propositions which are neither provable nor disprovable within the system; that is, the system cannot be complete. Menas Kafatos and Robert Nadeau have put it this way:

> "Gödel's enormously important but often ignored theorem...'proves' that mathematics, or the language of physical theory, cannot reach closure. Since no algorithm, or calculational procedure, that uses mathematical proofs can prove its own validity, any mathematical description which claims to have reached closure, or to have provided an exhaustively complete description of any aspect of physical reality, cannot prove itself... This means, in short, that even if we do construct a 'Theory of Everything', and even if that theory could somehow coordinate within its mathematical framework an explanation of life and/or consciousness, this theory could not 'in principle' claim to be a complete, final, or ultimate description."[92]

Gödel's Incompleteness Theorem arose out of an investigation of *Russell's Paradox*, which has to do with a branch of mathematics that is known as set theory. Russell's Paradox deals with a particular type of set, namely, sets which are not members of themselves. If we designate such types of set by the letter "R", then "R" can be defined as *the set of all sets which are not members of themselves.*

As Roger Penrose explains, if "R" is a certain collection of sets "X", then the criterion for a set "X" to belong to this collection is that the set "X" is not itself to be found among its own members. Penrose asks:

"How is it, then, that Russell's conception gives us a paradox?" Here is the reason why. "We ask, is Russell's very set "R" a member of itself, or is it not? If it is *not* a member of itself, then it should belong to "R", since "R" consists precisely of those sets which are not members of themselves. Thus "R" belongs to "R" after all—a contradiction. On the other hand, if "R" *is* a member of itself, then since 'itself' is actually "R", it belongs to that set whose members are characterized by *not* being members of themselves, i.e. it is not a member of itself after all—again, a contradiction!"[93]

A rather interesting illustration of this paradox that I have run across concerns a librarian who is asked to compile a complete catalog of all the books in the library. When he finishes the task, he decides not to include the catalog itself in the listing. Simultaneously, similar efforts are underway at other libraries, none of which include the finished catalogs themselves among the books listed. Suppose, now, that all these catalogs are collected into a single *supercatalog*, representing a superset of all the library catalogs that have been compiled which do not include themselves. How is this supercatalog to be regarded?

Call this supercatalog "R", as in Russell's Paradox, above. This supercatalog is thus the set of all sets which are not members of themselves. Now, if the supercatalog "R" is regarded as *not* a member of itself, then it cannot avoid *being* a member of itself, since it satisfies the conditions of membership which are, paradoxically, *non-membership*. On the other hand, if the supercatalog "R" is to be regarded as a bona fide member of itself, then it *cannot* be a member by the same paradoxical reasoning, since it contravenes the conditions of membership. The dilemma is plain. The supercatalog "R" must be regarded as *neither* a member *nor* a non-member of itself—an impossible contradiction!

Many prominent mathematicians, including Russell himself, spent years attempting to solve the riddle when Gödel shattered their dreams with one blow by showing that it couldn't be done. By demonstrating conclusively that there simply are a number of *undecidable propositions* in mathematics that lie outside the bounds of any formal algorithm, Gödel not only made himself very unpopular with certain of his colleagues but he also provided an unassailable argument that *no* physical theory based on mathematics can ever be complete. There will always be some truths that cannot be caught in the net of any theory, no matter how complex and comprehensive it may be. This, from my perspective, is Gödel's unique contribution to mathematics and the search for a 'final' physical theory. That search, I am convinced, cannot succeed, not only by the logic of Gödel's argument, but also by the strength of the convictions which many prominent physicists have voiced against it.

So where does this leave us with respect to a new quantum ontology? Just about where Bohm left us at his untimely death in 1992. Bohm had strongly hinted at some sort of metaphysical reality beyond physics, which he called the ultimate "ground" that gave rise to everything else, but he, too, was of the opinion that this *ground* could never be completely known. Although great strides have been made in physics during the present century, there is still no overall agreement on what constitutes physical 'reality'. It is Jim Baggott's contention that:

"No matter what the state of experimental science, the conflict between the positivists' conception of an empirical reality and the realists' conception of an *independent* reality can *never* be resolved... Any plea for an independent reality is really an appeal to faith, in the sense that the realist must ultimately accept the logic of the positivists' argument [that scientific knowledge is necessarily empirical] but will still not be persuaded." (Thus) "Three centuries of gloriously successful physics have brought us right back to the kind of speculation that it took three centuries of philosophy to reject as meaningless."[94]

What all of this strongly suggests is that there exists another reality, a realm beyond physics, which is the *metaphysical*, and of which the non-local interconnectedness exhibited by the quantum world is a reflection. My thesis is, in fact, that there exist *two* realms, side by side, so-to-speak, which for want of a better description I simply refer to as the material and the *noetic*. Noetic means "of or pertaining to the mind or the intellect" and which, in my use of the term, also includes spirit. We—we humans—are the experiencers, and the reality we experience *is* the noetic. David Bohm has hinted at the existence of the noetic realm in his exploration of the *plenum* or the eternal *ground*, but physicists have, until recently, been extremely reluctant to include the world of the mind, or the phenomenon of consciousness, in their explorations, because it represents a *discontinuity* of such proportions in their traditional reductionist ways of thinking as to constitute, in strictly scientific terms, a monstrous improbability. Yet it is a commonplace to all of us (physicists included!) when we are simply *experiencing* our lives instead of attempting to analyze them.

The physical world, the world of matter, which is, to some, so menacingly 'out there', and in which we are (again, by some) supposed to have been thrown up by the most ludicrous 'chance', is—as I have been at pains to demonstrate—a most ephemeral world in terms of any reductionist type of scientific analysis. When we have investigated the sub-atomic world of matter down to its smallest detail we find—nothing—only a seething vacuum of fields, energy, and 'virtual' particles, flitting into and out of existence. But surely there must be some connection between this mysterious ephemeral world by which we feel so threatened and the rich spiritual world of our mental and emotional experiences. It is the latter which is by far the most 'real' to us, rather than the distant and incomprehensible world of the quantum. What is this connection, the connection between the material and the noetic, which looms so tantalizingly, yet so unfathomably, before us?

In the quotation at the head of this chapter I noted Max Planck's observation that science cannot solve the ultimate mystery of nature because we, ourselves, are so integral a part of it.

We are both observed and observers, and in trying to look inside our own brains to see where the real self resides *we are missing the whole point. Mind is not identical to the brain, but is a separate reality.* The entire noetic realm of our experience is not identical to that which is experienced, but is a reflection of it. Indeed, I would turn the proposition around. It is conscious mind which *creates* the physical reality we experience. Mind is the creator of matter; matter is not the creator of mind. Mind is primary, and the world of matter could literally not exist without it!

If you find this proposition hard to swallow, consider what meaning there could possibly be to an unperceived universe. Ponder the question for a moment, and I think you will agree with me that there could be *no* meaning, because meaning is a value judgment, a concept involving perception, so that where there is no perception there is also no meaning. Well, then, did not the universe exist for billions of years before we happened upon the scene? Cosmologists assure us that it did, but this 'fact' had meaning only after it was consciously perceived. What is the meaning of a play before empty benches? Is an unperceived 'reality' yet 'real'? The whole thrust of orthodox quantum theory argues that it is not, that an objective reality arises only in the context of a measurement involving a conscious observer. The entire universe, then, in the view of some physicists, could not have existed (cosmologists notwithstanding!) until we came along. There is something a little self-consciously arrogant about all this, however. Philosophers and theologians have suggested that, perhaps, the Creator himself is the original observer and sustainer. It is the old problem of the tree falling in the forest when there is no one around to hear it. Does it then make a noise? It disturbs the air, but this cannot be the same thing as the perception of sound itself. The actual sound perception exists only in a perceiving mind. What about the soundwaves themselves? Can we accord them any sort of reality status, or are they also just a mental construct?

This whole question of what is real reminds me of Poul Anderson's comment that he had yet to see any problem, however complicated, which when you looked at it in the right way did not become still more complicated. The spirit/matter problem, which finds a parallel in the mind/body problem, has been debated throughout history. No one has yet solved it, but to my way of thinking Descartes' philosophy of *dualism* points in the right direction. Dualism finds a respectable echo in Bohr's notion of *complementarity* and in the mystery of the wave/particle dichotomy. The legendary physiologist, Sir Charles Sherrington, was fond of saying: "That our being should consist of two fundamental elements offers...no greater inherent improbability than that it should rest on one alone.[95] I shall have much more to say on this later.

For the moment I simply want to emphasize this important point, namely, that the world of our experience is the mental, the emotional, and the spiritual—what I call the *noetic*—and that all of this is experienced in the conscious mind. The eternal paradox is that our noetic world is vouchsafed to us only through its opposite, the physical and the material. It is in the world of matter that the world of spirit is reified, that is, made real. The two realms are as interlocked as the wave/particle duality; one literally cannot exist without the other, because neither can be *experienced* without the other. Both are complementary aspects of a single reality, the reality that David Bohm, as well as many others, have called the *eternal ground.*

This *eternal ground,* or *plenum,* is what David Bohm has also called the *holomovement,* and what in Buddhism is identified as *Brahman,* the Absolute Principle of all existence.[96] It is this which is transcendent and primary, which manifests itself in the material, and which is then reified, or experienced, in the noetic. We are thus part of a single totality, which is both spiritual and material, and which cannot be understood in terms of a reductionist analysis of its constituent parts, but is an unanalyzable whole, which is the same conclusion that most physicists have arrived at in their study of the quantum world.

A sense of awareness of this larger reality exists, I think, in every human being whether the individual openly acknowledges it or not. I do not believe that the sense of belonging to a larger whole is simply an 'emergent' property of the brain, but reflects the fact that the universe itself is probably conscious, as Bohm's conception of the *plenum* suggests it is. In this view it is not the individual atoms which are conscious, no more than the individual cells of the brain, but the whole universe of which the individual atoms constitute only a fleeting and evanescent part. In *The Compasses of God* I gave the analogy of the brain as a sort of radio receiver, all of whose parts must be specifically organized and in good working order if the receiver is to be able to extract from the surrounding medium the meaningful messages encoded on the radio waves of the electromagnetic fields which are everywhere present. Electromagnetic fields carrying radio waves have always existed in the universe, but they have not always carried messages. Only when the necessary technology was developed did it become possible to harness them for man's use, so that the analogy of the brain as a developing receiving instrument for an external source of consciousness may not be altogether implausible. In terms of Bohm's quantum ontology, consciousness was always *enfolded* in the universe and was *unfolded*, or rendered explicit, via the development of a suitable receiving instrument, the human brain.

The notion that the universe may itself be conscious is one that has been extensively developed by Menas Kafatos and Robert Nadeau, and it is one which finds an extraordinary echo in the following selection from Erwin Schrödinger's writings[97]:

> "Suppose you are sitting on a bench beside a path in high mountain country. There are grassy slopes all around, with rocks thrusting through them; on the opposite slope of the valley there is a stretch of scree with a low growth of alder bushes. Woods climb steeply on both sides of the valley, up to the line of treeless pasture; and facing you, soaring up from the depths of the valley, is the mighty glacier-tipped peak, its smooth snow fields and hard-edged rock faces touched at this moment by the last rays of the departing sun, all marvelously

sharp against the clear, pale, transparent blue of the sky.

"According to our usual way of looking at it, everything that you are seeing has, apart from small changes, been there for thousands of years before you. After a while—not long—you will no longer exist, and the woods and rocks and sky will continue, unchanged, for thousands of years after you.

"What is it that has called you so suddenly out of nothingness to enjoy for a brief while a spectacle which remains quite indifferent to you? The conditions for your existence are almost as old as the rocks. For thousands of years men have striven and suffered and begotten and women have brought forth in pain. A hundred years ago, perhaps, another man sat on this spot; like you he gazed with awe and yearning in his heart at the dying light on the glaciers. Like you he was begotten of man and born of woman. He felt pain and brief joy as you do. *Was* he someone else? Was it not you, yourself? What is this Self of yours? What was the necessary condition for making the thing conceived this time into *you*, just *you*, and not someone else? What clearly intelligible *scientific* meaning can this 'someone else' really have? If she who is now your mother had cohabited with someone else and had a son by him, and your father had done likewise, would *you* have come to be? Or, were you living in them, and in your father's father, ...thousands of years ago? And even if this is so, why are you not your brother, why is your brother not you, why are you not one of your distant cousins? What justifies you in obstinately discovering this difference—the difference between you and someone else—when objectively what is there is *the same?*

"Looking and thinking in that manner you may suddenly come to see, in a flash, ...that it is not possible that this unity of knowledge, feeling, and choice which you call *your own* should have sprung into being from nothingness at a given moment not so long ago; rather, this knowledge, feeling, and choice are essentially eternal and unchangeable and numerically *one* in all men, nay in all sensitive beings... Inconceivable as it seems to ordinary reason, you—and all other conscious beings as such—are all in all. Hence this life of yours which you are living is not merely a piece of the entire existence, but is in a certain sense the *whole;*... This, as we know, is what the Brahmins express in that sacred, mystic formula *Tat tvam asi*, this is you. Or, again, in such words as 'I am in the east and in the west, I am below and above. *I am this whole world.*'

"Thus you can throw yourself flat on the ground, stretched out upon Mother Earth, with the certain conviction that you are one with her and she with you. You are as firmly established, as invulnerable as she. As surely as she will engulf you tomorrow, so surely will she bring you forth anew to new striving and suffering. And not merely 'some day': now, today, every day she is bringing you forth, not *once* but thousands upon thousands of times, just as every day she engulfs you a thousand times over. For eternally and always there is only *now*, one and the same now; the present is the only thing that has no end."[98]

Wow! What a powerful thought! "The present is the only thing that has no end." The idea that there may really be only one "now" and one "self" is simply mind-blowing. This is not an idea that can be absorbed with equanimity. It upsets one's instinctive ideas of the nature of time and of the individual, but it deserves a respectful hearing. It is hard for the mind to conceive that there may be only this continuing *now*, a moment that is differently perceived by different observers and which cannot, therefore, be unequivocally identified. The reason it cannot be so identified is that every *now* is a strictly *local* experience, which is dependent on the speed of light, thus making it impossible for everyone's 'now' to be the same. This will be attested to by anyone who has ever conducted a long distance telephone conversation. Over long distances small overlaps in the conversation are found to occur because the voice transmission cannot be simultaneous. There literally is no such thing as a universal *now* that can be perceived as such by two distant observers. We are reminded of Zeno's paradox, where time is conceived of as a succession of infinitely short 'nows', but where the manner in which the future becomes the past is no more explainable than the manner in which a series of closely juxtaposed points becomes a line.

Schrödinger's perception that the present moment is unending suggests that 'now' is literally an eternal moment, not a moment in time, which is a different thing. Man participates in this eternal moment and ceases to participate in it at death. In Schrödinger's vision the death of an individual is not to be dreaded because the self is indestructible; it lives in all of us. In Schrödinger's opinion the difference between me and my brother—or anyone else—"has no clearly intelligible *scientific* meaning." This statement, if correct, would compel one to conclude that, in fact, there *is* no difference, except what has been dictated by genetics and accumulated personal experience. The self, Schrödinger has indicated, is merely the "canvas" on which such experiences are "collected". This, however, is a view that in the West does not go down easily. The western, Judeo-Christian view is that there is a 'soul' in the body that constitutes the essence of the self and which, in the opinion of famed neuroscientist, Sir John Eccles, "is a divine creation." If the self is an illusion, then we must quite literally abandon hope, for, as Stanley Jaki has put it, "Unless one takes one's certainty of the immediately perceived reality as the primary safe ground, no ground will be left for safely retaining any reality, let alone the reality of the universe."[99]

My point of view is a dualistic one, a perspective that Schrödinger is reluctant to consider. Following the lead of Descartes, I find that I cannot deny my own existence. I am convinced of the reality of my own 'soul', notwithstanding the fact that science recognizes no such thing. But science ought to be our servant, not our master. Dualism offers us a way out of the dilemma of self by postulating mind and body as separate entities which stand in a logically reciprocal relationship to one another. *Mind needs matter to give it expression, while matter needs mind to give it meaning.* Dualism is an ancient and honorable philosophy which finds a parallel in Bohr's *complementarity* as well as in the venerable Chinese notion of *t'ai-chi.*

My own view of this has already been indicated. I see no insurmountable difficulty in postulating a selfhood that is consonant with the existence of a universal consciousness. Schrödinger's statement that "no intelligible scientific meaning" attaches to this notion might be said of much of quantum mechanics. Awareness of self is that which is *most real* to us, and it would be foolish to ignore this fundamental fact. Our material brains and bodies, which are genetically distinct, are not simply clones of one another, and I see nothing outrageous in postulating a self which, while identified with these brains and bodies, receives its *self-awareness* from a universal consciousness that envelops it, much as everything material is enveloped by a constant ebb and flow of electromagnetic fields filling all time and space and whose energy equivalent is so succinctly expressed in Einstein's famous $E=MC^2$. Might it not be that consciousness is simply another form or manifestation of this universal energy, said to be found even in the vacuum, and that it is as fundamental a reality of the universe as the equivalence of matter and energy itself?

More of this in the next chapter, where the reality of the conscious self is more deeply explored. What I have tried to show here, in touching on some mysteries beyond physics, is that there does exist a kind of "veiled reality", in Bernard d'Espagnat's phrase, behind the facade of ordinary physics. I do not believe that we will ever be able to completely lift this veil or that we shall come up with a 'final theory', but it is nevertheless fascinating to speculate about it. Informed speculation is often the handmaiden of scientific progress and, if there is any real purpose to the universe then it is not only legitimate but perhaps inevitable that we should speculate about it.

SIXTEEN

THE PERSONIFICATION OF SELF

"My one regret in life is that I'm not someone else."
–Woody Allen

I said in the last chapter, "If the self is an illusion, then we must quite literally abandon hope..." Why is belief in the reality of self so vital?

There are a number of reasons. First and foremost, I would say, is that when we devalue the self, we devalue all human experience. The most outstanding example of this in our society today is the prevalence of abortion. Whatever justification there may be for this practice, there is no gainsaying the fact that abortion is the denial of life. The plain fact is that abortion is the killing of a human fetus, a fetus whose biological origin and development is perhaps the greatest miracle of creation. When we fiercely defend our own right to exist while denying it to those who come after us, we are guilty of the worst form of hypocrisy.

Actually, we are guilty of far more than that. When we devalue life, we undermine the entire moral structure of civilization. The systematic devaluation of others' right to exist is a *sine qua non* of warfare. In peacetime it encourages an increase in crime and a general disrespect for law and order. We have witnessed the terrible consequences of the devaluation of life and of the self in Hitler's holocaust and in the Stalinist tyranny, and we are daily witnessing it in the increasing amount of terrorism around the globe. If there is one thing that discourages me from faith in progress, it is the failure of the human race to learn from history. And I am convinced that at the root of this failure is the persistent devaluing of the notion of self and of Albert Schweitzer's "reverence for life", most particularly in our own century.

The undermining of the notion of reverence for life has been fostered in the modern era by such sterile philosophies as radical positivism and behaviorism, both of which have demeaned the view that there is any deeper significance to life than what is evidenced empirically and behaviorally. Thankfully, these philosophies have now lost a great deal of their influence, but they have been replaced, in part, by an obsession with biology and genetics as the touchstone for 'explaining' what the human being is all about. Yet biologists and neuroscientists, for all their diligence, have not been able to locate the self in the body nor the mind in the brain. Failing to find them there, they have declared them absent and their assumed reality an illusion.

I submit, however, that the last thing any of us feels comfortable with is the idea of declaring himself to be an illusion. No one really believes this of himself, not even such vehement anti-religionists as Peter Atkins, a lecturer in physical chemistry at Oxford, who has uttered such nonsense as: "All the extraordinary, wonderful richness of the world can be expressed as growth from the dunghill of purposeless interconnected corruption."[100] We all believe, on the contrary, that we are 'real' and that the world is 'real', or else most of us would not bother to get up in the morning. All of our planning, our hopes, our work, our purposeful dedication and sacrifice would seem to be for naught if we could not believe in the reality of our own lives and the lives of others.

In *Mind and Matter*, one of the Tarner Lectures that Schrödinger delivered at Trinity College, Oxford, in 1956, the inventor of wave mechanics spoke movingly of the mysterious dichotomy between mind and body with which we are all acquainted. Schrödinger noted that, in the human body,

> "...we find millions of cells of very specialized build in an arrangement that is unsurveyably intricate but quite obviously serves a very far-reaching and consummate mutual communication and collaboration; a ceaseless hammering of regular electrochemical pulses which, however, change rapidly in their configuration, being conducted from nerve cell to nerve cell, tens of thousands of contacts being opened and blocked within every split second, chemical transformations being induced... Now let us assume that in a particular case you eventually observe several efferent bundles of pulsating currents, which issue from the brain and through long cellular protrusions (motor nerve fibers) are conducted to certain muscles of the arm which, as a consequence, tends a hesitating, trembling hand to wish you farewell—for a long, heart-rending separation; at the same time you may find that some other pulsating bundles produce a certain glandular secretion so as to veil the poor sad eye with a crape of tears. But nowhere along this way, nowhere, you may be sure, however far physiology advances—will you ever meet the personality, will you ever meet the dire pain, the bewildered worry within this soul, though their reality is to you so certain as though you suffered them yourself—as in actual fact you do!"

Schrödinger goes on to note that:

> "The material world has only been constructed at the price of taking the self out of it... The reason why our sentient, percipient, and thinking ego is

met nowhere within our scientific world picture is...*because it is itself that world picture.* It is identical with the whole and therefore cannot be contained in it as a part of it."[101] [italics mine]

Schrödinger clearly does not think that the self can be located inside the body, but he appears to share with the philosophy of *Vedanta* [in which he was a confirmed believer] the notion that we are all somehow one with 'the great ocean of being'. The illusion of self, if I have interpreted him correctly, stems from our acquaintance with a multiplicity of *bodies*, whereas Schrödinger believes that there is really only one universal self, one consciousness, that resides in all these bodies. As evidence he notes that "Consciousness is never experienced in the plural, only in the singular", by which he appears to mean that none of us ever experiences more than one consciousness. "Even in cases of split personality", he notes, "the two persons alternate, they never hold the field jointly."[102] Schrödinger's attraction to eastern mysticism is apparently also responsible for his provocative suggestion that the man gazing across the mountain valley in the passage I have cited is one and the same with another who contemplated the scene a hundred years ago. His belief in the oneness of self clearly expresses itself in the thought: "What justifies you in obstinately discovering this difference—the difference between you and someone else—when objectively what is there is *the same?*"[103]

I must say that I find the Vedantist view uncongenial, for a number of reasons, one of which has to do with the fact that the world obviously harbors examples of extreme diversity in personality among men. It is apparent to me that I am not the same person as my brother. On the other hand, I have to acknowledge the force of Schrödinger's observation about the unity of "true lovers who, as they look into each other's eyes, become aware that their thoughts and their joys are *numerically* one—not merely similar or identical."[104]

Nevertheless, Schrödinger has posed a profound question in asking why I am not my brother, a distant cousin, or "someone else". This touches on the central mystery: Why was the 'thing' born this time *me* and not *you?*

To answer this riddle, if an answer is indeed possible, let us consider, first of all, what happens in the biological process of conception and why one human being differs from another.

When a baby is conceived there is, as everyone knows, a biological fusion of the sex cells of male and female, of father and mother. Now, the sex cells of the human body are unique: They are not the same as the ordinary cells of the body, which are basically similar, consisting of a 'bag' of fluid inside a very thin membrane containing a central dark nucleus. The process by which the sex cells, egg and sperm, are formed is different from that of ordinary cells. Ordinary cell division (mitosis) makes exact copies of itself; this is how growth occurs. Sex cell production (meiosis), on the other hand, makes cells that are *not identical* to one another. During meiosis "chunks of chromosomes are broken apart, swapped between the pairs, and recombined into new arrangements... There is a constant re-shuffling of the genetic pack...it is this which accounts for the astonishing amount of variability among individual members of species that reproduce sexually."[105] *Meiosis* in both males and females produces cells that contain only 23 chromosomes—half the full complement of 46 which are carried by each ordinary (non-sex) human cell. In the female sex cell (the ovum) one of these 23 chromosomes is markedly different from the rest, and is called "X". The same is true of the male, but in the male the different chromosome may be *either* "X" or "Y". When fusion of sperm and egg (ovum) occur during conception, *either* an "X" or a "Y" chromosome of the male [in addition to the other 22 the male sperm carries] unites with an "X" chromosome of the female [together with the female's additional complement of 22] to produce *either* a female or a male *zygote*—the technical name for the fertilized ovum. Thus it is that the father decides the sex of the child; the mother's ovum is *always* female, containing only "X" chromosomes. The father's sperm, on the other hand, contains *either* "X" or "Y". Therefore, roughly 50% of all births will be male, while the other 50% will be female. That is *one* important source of the difference between human beings.

But if that were the only difference, all females would still be clones of one another, as would all males. The rest of the difference, at least genetically, is accounted for by the re-shuffling of the genetic pack during meiosis in both males and females. This makes it virtually *impossible* for any two male sperm or any two female eggs to be the same, and thus it is that their union will always produce a *unique* individual.

However, we all know that identical twins occur, and even higher orders of multiple birth. Genetically, these *have to be the same*, because they all result from a single zygote when the attached cells become separated from one another. Fraternal twins, in contrast, result from the cleavage of *two* zygotes. Yet "Even identical twins with identical genes will not have identical brains at birth; the fine details of cortical circuitry will be quite different."[106] It is also apparent that they do not possess the *same* consciousness, since they do not react as one to the same stimuli. As they mature, of course, they turn out to be remarkably alike, although never identical, as might be suggested by the conditions of their conception. What, then, makes each of them *unique?*

The only conceivable answer—to me—is that "something else has been added". That 'something else' is, I believe, a 'divine spark' or 'soul' that is part of the mysterious process which we call human life. Unless this is so, I do not see how Schrödinger's conclusion can be avoided. Schrödinger's conclusion is that the self is merely the "canvas" upon which each person's experiences are "collected". The self, in this view, 'emerges' from a pattern of genetic chemistry and a bundle of 'experiences' and is different from other selves only in these two essential respects. There is then nothing to celebrate or to value uniquely in the self, because the self is nothing but a chance combination of genes over whose assembly and subsequent development we had no control. I find this view so depressing and dismal that I simply cannot share Schrödinger's joy, in the lengthy paragraph I quoted, at being "engulfed" by Mother Earth, and then being brought forth, in endless variety, again and again. The 'me' that is being reborn in Schrödinger's conception is not a 'me' that I can empathize or identify with, but simply another chemical pattern, the result of blind chance.

If this chemical notion of the self is correct, and there is indeed only *one* consciousness that resides in all of us, there is no hope for a resurrection in which we shall meet our loved ones ever again. If we are just random combinations of genetic material, there can be no permanent reality to our existence, any more than there is a permanent reality to the rainbow which—though uniquely produced—is a transient phenomenon reflecting basically similar atmospheric conditions. I do not wish to be interpreted here as an apologist for Christian dogma, I simply want to emphasize the absolute irreconcilability of the chemical notion of self with the idea of the Soul, which has always underlain most western philosophy. It seems to me that if we abandon the idea of Soul, of a unique Self or Spirit that is the essence of our being, then we are left with the vacuous and unsatisfying 'great ocean of being' philosophy of the eastern religions, at best, and with the utter collapse of any inspirational theology, at worst. We are left with the view that man, and life in general, is a mere epiphenomenon in a universe of chance, to which no meaning can be attached, and that his fate is sealed by the inevitability of the Second Law of Thermodynamics. Such a view, however fanatically defended by some, is anathema to me, because I feel "in my bones", as Einstein was wont to say, that it is *incomplete.* There must be more to man's reality than this, or the Great Playwright and Designer of the cosmic drama would have delivered himself of a very poor production, indeed.

Life itself is the central mystery. In his 1985 book *In Search of the Double Helix* John Gribben writes as follows:

"The puzzle of life is the puzzle of how the fusion of one unusually large cell, the egg, with another smaller cell, the sperm, can result in a single cell which proceeds through a series of complex stages to divide into first two, then four, and eventually a great many cells, not at random but through a series of stages in which folds, buckles, and indentations form and develop as the bundle of cells grows, eventually taking on the adult form."[107]

Cell division and growth is a process that no biologist has been able to explain, except to note the mechanics thereof. Utterly mysterious is the process by which the newly-formed cells become smaller in size and begin to organize themselves according to some apparent 'master plan'. Here, pre-eminently, it is obvious that there exist fundamental laws of form and design that remain to be discovered. How do the newly-created cells, which are superficially all alike, 'know' where to go to build the adult structure? How do these blobs of protoplasm organize themselves into a brain, which then becomes introspectively aware of itself? Is it conceivable that all this can be due to 'chance', the result of the "efflorescence" of Atkins' "dunghill"?

I do not believe it. Neuroscientist Sir John Eccles, a Nobel prizewinner, has opined that "each self is a divine creation." The uniqueness of self is anchored in the fact that, as Schrödinger has noted, consciousness is never encountered in the plural. Although Schrödinger used this fact to undergird his theory of a *single* consciousness, I find it supportive of the fact that in a material world a multiplicity of bodies requires a multiplicity of selves, because no single self or body can be ubiquitous. But why is the self in *my* body 'me' rather than 'you'?

I don't think the answer is any more scientifically determinable than why a single electron travels through hole "A" rather than hole "B" in Young's double-slit experiment, or why *this* probability rather than another is selected when a quantum observation is made. In a sense the question dissolves into a semantic one because we are all "me's" to ourselves but "you's" to one another. In this respect Schrödinger is quite right that no *scientifically* intelligible meaning attaches to the question. But I do not conclude from this that the self in each of us is an illusion; I prefer the Eccles response, to the effect that each self is a divine creation. I am powerfully persuaded, as I feel certain you are, too, that I am *not* an illusion, although the briefness of my sojourn on this earth, seen against the backdrop of eternity, might appear to be no more real than the 'reality' we accord to a 'virtual' particle. Moreover, I am not the *same* as everyone else. There is no compelling reason why all reflections of a universal consciousness should be identical. My mind is not the *same* as your mind, though sometimes we share similar thoughts. Whenever we *do* share the same thought, perhaps in sharing a moment of laughter or bliss, the poignancy of that moment, I submit, resides in the fact that we are *not* one but *separate* reflections of what we may postulate as a universal consciousness. For the essence of sharing lies in the polarity of oneness *versus* separateness; there can be no sense of sharing without an "other" to share an experience with. My answer to Schrödinger, then, is that the *sharing* of our lives and our thoughts with others who may be like us but who are not identical is what gives life its fullness and its richness and makes it all worth while. Not to be able to share life with another self would rob it of its essential meaning. The Bible indicates that even Adam needed a "helpmeet". That is why I am, fundamentally, a dualist. I reject the notion of only a single self for the same reason that I reject the Vedanta striving after dissolution of the ego in some mystical union with Brahman. I have always felt such a striving to be arid and sterile and even, ultimately, selfish.

The English philosopher, E.W.F. Tomlin, has written movingly on this theme:

> "Love...implies the kind of relationship which Martin Buber has defined as that of 'I' and 'Thou', as opposed to 'I and it'. 'When shall I be free?', asks Ramakrishna. 'When the 'I' has vanished.' But if the 'I' has vanished altogether, how is the love relationship possible, and what is meant by being free? There must be something for me to give, even if only to give up: and the paradox of love is that, in such giving up, the self increases in stature. Only the self that is incapable of such sacrifice remains

sterile, a self-centered ego. On the plane of meta-physics, the Buddhist and Vedanta injunction to destroy the ego as a preliminary to merging with the Absolute is first to effect a cancellation, and then to propel a zero to infinity... According to Vedanta teaching, what is uncovered when the ego is canceled is the *Atman;* and *Atman* is one with *Brahman*...but if there is no sacrifice, merely an annulment, there can be no merit... But we do exist; and the aim of philosophy is not so much to destroy existence as to render it significant."[108]

Tomlin's conclusion, namely, that the aim of philosophy should be to render life significant, is one with which I can fully agree. It seems to me that a philosophy of dualism, of the recognition of opposites, encompasses its essence. Perhaps I should emphasize instead Bohr's notion of *complementarity,* for it is not the extremeness of opposites that I want to stress, but the joining of similar, though different, perspectives.[109] The sharing of experiences when one self momentarily merges into another is invaluable in teaching us, not that we are all the *same,* but that the *other* is as precious and important a being as ourselves. Only this realization can enable us to break out of our natural sollipsism which, unless vehemently resisted, strives every day to persuade us that our own ego is the center of the universe. The realization that it is not may come as a shock or as a release. The prospect of our own death is one that is feared mostly because of our self-centeredness. The experience of wholly 'finding' ourselves in another teaches us, as nothing else can, that our own demise is less significant than we would like to think, for it is fully compensated by the ongoing lives of equally valuable 'others'. We may fear, but we do not mourn, our own deaths. The mourning is felt by the ones we leave behind, as the bond which one human soul shares with another is, at least physically, severed.

The fascination of a pluralistic universe lies, I find, in the paradox that every person who has ever existed was, in a sense, 'me'.

The world can only be experienced, so-to-speak, one at a time, from the perspective of millions of different 'me's', and each perspective is unique. The beauty of it all is that, in 'finding' ourselves in another, the wonder of this universe can be shared and the life of each individual 'me' incalculably enriched.

A philosophy of dualism, or of complementarity if you prefer, is therefore essential, to my way of thinking, in order to render possible the most beautiful and the most rewarding of life's experiences, namely, the *sharing* of life's joys and burdens with a beloved 'other'. That is why, in my opinion, separate 'selves' exist in a world in which everything else is also an expression of the necessary unity of opposites. Although we often idealize unity, it is one of the paradoxes of this ideal that the existence of opposites, of different selves, is required to achieve it.

There remains the question of what sort of 'reality' can be accorded the personal 'I' after its material underpinnings have returned to dust. It should strike us as somewhat odd that we seldom pose the same question with respect to the eons which passed before our birth. Where were we during those eons, and why are we not equally concerned with them?

It is an interesting question, as well as a provocative one. We are afraid of death because our temporal mind-sets find the immensity of 'eternity' intimidating. We are not concerned with a previous existence because we have no memory of one. Schrödinger thought that birth was like awakening from a long sleep, during which our memories had been "erased". But if "The present is the only thing that never ends", then it is always the present when we re-awaken. We can remember the past and imagine the future, but we can really only *live* in the present. Consciousness exists only in the present. What is there in all of this to be afraid of?

Is it really conceivable that our souls may be eternal, even though we may not be aware of time's passing when we have no body? Quite as conceivable, I would think, as to believe in the reality of a quantum world that we can neither see, touch, taste, or feel but can only detect through our measuring instruments, and then only in the most indirect way. We do not consider the cosmos to be an illusion simply because it rests on a foundation of ceaselessly fluctuating and evanescent particles, none of which have any 'real' attributes or separate existence except in our mathematics. Why, then, do we find the notion of our reality as a spiritual entity so strange? It seems to me perfectly conceivable to oppose the notion of matter with the notion of spirit (mind), the one requiring the other for their mutual expression. It is only when we make the *ontological* reality of spirit dependent on the presence of matter that we run into difficulty, but *that*, I am convinced, is putting the cart before the horse.

When our material bodies have returned to dust, the physical instrument through which our spirits are able to "tune in" to the consciousness that floods the universe will no longer exist, temporarily cutting the 'connection'. However, there will be other participants, other 'me's', who will still be 'hooked up', and not just on planet Earth, because it is likely that conscious beings exist throughout the universe. This, of course, is highly speculative but widely hypothesized by many members of the scientific community. One 'day', perhaps, it will be 'our turn' again to participate, and the possibility that eons may have passed before we are again consciously aware will be of no consequence in a timeless eternity.

Is there, in Schrödinger's phrase, any "clearly intelligible scientific meaning" to this prospect and to the persistence of an eternal soul?

The only honest answer to that question must be in the negative. However, as we have seen, science has no monopoly on truth and is, in the last analysis, incapable of encompassing the ultimate [Gödel]. Furthermore, science is continually deepening and enlarging its perspectives on what constitutes ultimate reality, as we have seen from our historical survey. If there are non-local influences pervasive in a universe which is constantly "enfolding" and "unfolding" in an infinite manifestation of its laws and principles, then why must we be timid about asserting as real and eternal the ontological verity of that with which we are most intimately acquainted, namely, our own existence? Science cannot 'prove' or 'disprove' anything, except a logical absurdity. It proceeds by trial and error and empirical verification to grope its way forward toward 'truth' in a vision that is forever changing. Our conscious presence in the universe at this moment in time is the only thing of which we can be absolutely certain. All the rest is faith, whether scientific, metaphysical, or religious. Our personal participation in the cosmic drama cannot be significant in the perspective of eternity, though it is all-in-all to us. The drama goes on in the minds of other participants until it is appropriate for us to make a renewed entrance upon the 'stage'. Will we play the same part in the performance as before? That would be hardly possible, as the play changes. But it is not inconceivable at all that we, the actors, will be the same. This is for me frankly a 'leap of faith', but I believe that I am as entitled to make it as any that scientists have adopted as their own. The history of science is replete with such leaps that have been taken, in each instance, to 'explain' what had not been explainable before.

A broader perspective is obtained by focusing on something to which I have previously alluded, namely, that the individual who is 'me' is a mirror image of the beloved 'other' whom we may have found in our peregrinations on planet Earth, and that both are equally precious and real in the eyes of eternity. From this perspective the importance of the material manifestation of our own ego becomes less relevant to the scheme of things, and we are willing to 'let go' of this world, when the time comes, secure and content in the certain knowledge that it is in equally good and capable hands. If we have experienced the loss, through death, of a beloved 'other' who was that mirror image, while his or her spirit continues to be reflected in our own, this fact can sometimes strengthen and deepen our conviction of the eternality of the soul.

In closing, I would like to cite Schrödinger's view of the self taken from his well-known *What is Life?*, originally published in 1944 and widely hailed by scientists and humanists alike for its insights:

"Each of us has the undisputable impression that the sum total of his own experience and memory forms a unit, quite distinct from that of any other person. He refers to it as "I". *What is this 'I'?*

"If you analyze it closely you will, I think, find that it is just a little bit more than a collection of single data (experiences and memories), namely, the canvas *upon which* they are collected. And you will, on close inspection, find that what you really mean by 'I' is that groundstuff upon which they are collected. You may come to a distant country, lose sight of all your friends, may all but forget them; you acquire new friends, you share life with them as intensely as you ever did with your old ones. Less and less important will become the fact that, while living your new life, you still recollect the old one. 'The youth that was I', you may come to speak of him in the third person, indeed, the protagonist of the novel you are reading is probably nearer to your heart, certainly more intensely alive and better known to you. Yet there has been no intermediate break, no death. And even if a skilled hypnotist succeeded in blotting out entirely all your earlier reminiscences, you would not find that he had killed *you*. In no case is there a loss of personal existence to deplore.

"Nor will there ever be."[110]

I find Schrödinger's poetic description stimulating, provocative, and somewhat mystical. Although I do not subscribe 100% to Schrödinger, there is in him an honesty of expression, a willingness to probe deeply, and a sense of humanity that is paralleled by few other scientific writers. In the end, it is up to each of us to decide for himself where the truth lies. That is essentially what I have tried to do for myself through these ruminations.

SEVENTEEN

MIND AND CONSCIOUSNESS

"Absence of evidence is not evidence of absence."
–M. Rees

In the previous chapter, *The Personification of Self*, I touched upon the phenomenon of consciousness which animates the human body and thus lends identifiable reality to the human self. I now want to pursue that theme further.

Scientists have traditionally avoided dealing with subjects like mind or consciousness because they could find no *physical* evidence of their existence in the body or in the neuronal network of the brain. All that they have ever been able to find in the human brain—that three-pound "wet computer" underneath our skulls—is an immensely complicated electrochemical circuitry which reacts in certain ways when prodded or stimulated but which has never been identified with mind or consciousness itself. There is an apparently unbridgeable dichotomy, a discontinuity of sorts, between brain and consciousness, or mind and body, about which physics or biology has little to say. Descartes' view that the two are separate entities has been unacceptable to most neuroscientists. Most of them have postulated either a theory of *identity* between mind and brain or a theory of *evolution* in which consciousness gradually developed in the brain over eons of time and was literally a reflection of the brain's *functioning*. This was the bedrock of logical positivist and behaviorist theories of mind and matter during the first half of the twentieth century. In these theories consciousness was dismissed as irrelevant, if not nonexistent. "Conscience has no observable referent...and is therefore meaningless", said logical positivist Burnham Beckwith.[111] "The nature of subjective experience" was "a minor problem soon to vanish", wrote behaviorist B.F. Skinner.[112] And, "It is not clear that the behavior of any individual or the course of world history would have been affected in any way if awareness were nonexistent...", declared logical positivist Dean Wooldridge.[113] This kind of nonsense, which viewed every mental activity strictly in stimulus-response terms, was rampant at mid-century when Roger Sperry, winner of the 1981 Nobel Prize for Medicine and Physiology, threw down the gauntlet to the materialists, whose only aim seemed to be to prove that "the idea of the mind as causal, so evident to all religions and to all philosophies previously", was a chimera and an illusion.[114]

Sperry, the 'father' of split-brain research, was at the height of his reputation as a neuroscientist when he began demolishing the positivist-behaviorist views which had brought further progress into the true nature of mind and consciousness virtually to a halt. Erika Erdmann, Dr. Sperry's library research assistant for almost ten years, writes of the development of Sperry's philosophy from 1965 on in the following terms:

> "The concepts of *emergence* and of *downward_causation* are central to the understanding of Sperry's philosophy. Every one of (Sperry's) papers on consciousness emphasizes two key postulates:
>
> 1. The mind, or *consciousness*, as an emergent property of brain function, interacts *causally* at its own mental level. In other words, mind emerges from matter, but mind interacts in mental terms—in terms of thought and ideas, not neural activities.

2. Consciousness exerts downward control over brain activity in an encompassing supervenient sense. In short, mind controls matter.

Or, expressed with the utmost simplicity:

Mind emerges from matter.
Thoughts and ideas interact at their own level.
Mind controls matter.

These ideas were obviously anathema to the behaviorists, but they gradually began to gain adherents. In Erdmann's words, "The crucial difference between Sperry and materialistic neuroscientists is that he sees mental interaction as a newly-emerged phenomenon of primary importance, with chemical changes being secondary; while materialists argue that events occur the other way around, with physical and chemical changes of first importance and mental action a superfluous by-product."[115]

I find it interesting that Erdmann describes Sperry's concept of *supervention* in much the same way that I have thought of the mind/consciousness/brain relationship, namely, in terms of the reception by a physical instrument, such as a television receiver, of information from an external source, that is, the television program, that controls the pattern of light and dark formed on the screen—an analogy said by Erdmann to have been used by Sperry in several of his papers. Erdmann and the co-author of her book, David Stover, have coined the term *emergent causation* for Sperry's unifying vision of the mind/ body relationship, "which involves the *supervenience*, or superimposing, of higher-order natural events onto lower-order ones (and which leaves physical interactions in the brain intact and untouched...)"[116]

Roger Sperry has rejected reductionism and has come up with a *holistic* theory of consciousness *emerging* from the brain and yet somehow controlling it in a non-material way. Erdmann and Stover are at pains to point out that Sperry's position is something intermediate between identity theory and outright dualism [of the Cartesian variety]. I agree, but would argue that the brain's holistic properties are more satisfactorily explained by a forthright acceptance of a Cartesian dualism rather than by an emergent process which cannot account for what or why something 'emerges'. The problem with Sperry's theory, in other words, is that it does not go far enough. The mystery of the origin of the alleged self-organizing or emergent properties of the brain remains unsolved and unaddressed. We might conclude from this philosophy that the entire universe has organized itself from nothingness in an ascending scale of complex and ultimately mental forms, but by what means and to what purpose? Does Sperry's concept of the emergence of mind from brain imply some sort of teleology? The doctrine of emergent causation circumvents the question. It recognizes the qualitative difference of conscious, directing, creative mind from matter, yet it asserts that the former has arisen mysteriously from the latter. Why this inversion? Why not assert mind's primacy and matter (brain) as the necessary vehicle for its expression? Sperry has indeed hinted at this with his television analogy, but it is my impression that he has failed to follow through.

Another Nobel Laureate, Sir John Eccles, whom Sperry influenced, has seized the nettle and has gone the whole distance. In the words of Judith Hooper and Dick Teresi, co-authors of *The Three-Pound Universe—The Brain,*

> "Eccles' gospel is basically a reincarnation of Descartes's, to wit, that 'We are a combination of two things, or entities: our brains, on the one hand, and our conscious selves on the other.' ...Eccles believes in a "ghost", a non-material (and immortal) soul animating the computer-like brain. In this view he echoes his former mentor at Oxford, the legendary physiologist Sir Charles Sherrington, who wrote: 'That our being should consist of two fundamental elements...offers no greater inherent improbability than that it should rest on one alone.'"[117]

The fact that three eminent authorities in the field of neuroscience agree that mind controls matter does not, of course, prove my case for dualism, but neither does it render that case wholly implausible. To me it is evident that mind is an *ontological reality* distinct from that warm three-pound porridge we call "the brain". The brain, with all its circuits in good working order, may be *ready to function* and to receive information, but—like an old tube radio which hums and glows when it has been turned on—it will remain silent unless there is also, surrounding it, an external source of energy of some kind. With respect to the radio this external source of energy is the electromagnetic field carrying the radio wave; with respect to the brain the external source is a universal field of consciousness. Both are realities that we assume to exist but can neither see, feel, nor touch. We *assume* the existence of electromagnetic fields in space to explain the transmission of light from the sun, and we *assume* the existence of gravitational fields to explain the orbital motions of the planets, but neither of these assumptions is a proven fact [See pages 110-111]. Why, then, do scientists find it so difficult to assume the existence of a universal field of consciousness?

A philosophy of dualism encompasses two ontological realities, mind and matter, but it accords a primacy to mind, the creator, which is *in control*. I can see no fundamental objection to it other than the visceral unwillingness of some die-hard reductionists to put first things first. Quantum mechanics should have shown us, if it has shown us anything, that it is the *whole* which governs the behavior of the parts and that it is via the whole that the parts are accorded whatever individual properties they are found, on observation, to 'possess'. The reality of the parts is literally dependent on the reality of the whole, which is their ontological *ground*. This is a view that, on the quantum level, few theoretical physicists today would wish to challenge. I ask again, why are so many socio-biologists unwilling to take a similar view of the conscious mind?

Physicist Roger Penrose has written: "Classical physics seems incapable of explaining a phenomenon so deeply mysterious as consciousness. The physical world we know is extremely mysterious, and the more we probe its foundations, the more mysterious it becomes." Nobel Laureate Gerald M. Edelman, Director of the Neurosciences Institute at San Diego, California, states emphatically: *"A person is not explainable in molecular, field-theoretical, or physiological terms alone—*to reduce a person's behavior to a theory of molecular interactions is simply silly...a theory of action based on the notion of human freedom appears to be receiving more and more support from the scientific facts."[118]

I find that a number of Edelman's ideas about time and consciousness run rather parallel to my own:

> "The sense of time is first and foremost a conscious event, (so that)...ideas of consciousness and 'experienced' time are...closely intertwined...the personal sense of the sacred, the sense of mystery, and the sense of ordering and continuity all have connections to temporal continuity as we experience it... This view of time is distinguishable from the relativistic clock-time used by physicists, which is...reversible... The brain is neither a machine nor the implementation of a computer program... human beings have a degree of free will...they can indulge in extraordinary imaginative freedom, and are obviously of a different order... They possess 'selfhood', shored up by emotions and higher-order consciousness."[119]

Roger Penrose has touched on a number of these same themes in *The Emperor's New Mind:*

> "Is it not obvious that mere computation cannot evoke pleasure or pain, that it cannot perceive poetry or the beauty of an evening sky; that it cannot hope or love or despair; that it cannot have a genuine autonomous purpose? Yet science seems to have driven us to accept that we are all merely small parts of a world governed in full detail...by very precise mathematical laws. Our brains themselves...are also ruled by these same precise laws.

The picture has emerged that all this precise physical activity is, in effect, nothing more than the acting-out of some vast, perhaps probabilistic, computation—and hence our brains and our minds are to be understood solely in terms of such computations... Yet it is hard to avoid an uncomfortable feeling that there must always be something missing from such a picture... Consciousness seems to me such an important phenomenon that I simply cannot believe that it is something just 'accidentally' conjured up by a complicated computation. It is the phenomenon whereby the universe's very existence is made known. One can argue that a universe governed by laws that do not allow consciousness is no universe at all... It is only the phenomenon of consciousness that can conjure a putative 'theoretical' universe into actual existence!"

The Emperor's New Mind concludes with the thought:

"In this book I have presented many arguments intending to show the untenability of the viewpoint...that our thinking is basically the same as the action of some very complicated computer... Beyond all this technicality (of a computer-like brain) is the feeling that it is indeed obvious that the *conscious* mind cannot work like a computer, even though what is actually involved in mental activity might do so."[120]

It should be clear from the foregoing that, whatever consciousness may be, it cannot be reduced to the concept of a "wet computer". Nor can it be explained, as Danah Zohar attempts to do, as some sort of quantum wave pattern on the Bose-Einstein concentrate in the brain, stemming from the "correlated jiggling of molecules in the neuron cell walls."[121] All reductionist hypotheses of this sort fail fundamentally to explain consciousness, because consciousness, as it is experienced, is qualitatively distinct from any such "jiggling". All reductionist theses are ultimately grounded in the belief that consciousness is an 'emergent' property of the brain that somehow arises 'naturally' when all the necessary constituent parts have been assembled.

On the other hand, it is also clear—so far as we know—that consciousness does not occur without a physical agency through which it can manifest itself, whether that agency be the human brain or the more primitive nervous systems of the lower creatures. All such physical systems require constant replenishment of the energies they put out, since all are subject to the Second Law of Thermodynamics, the law that all far-from-equilibrium isolated systems tend constantly to dissipate energy [See Chapter 18]. The Second Law manifests itself in the human brain and body through what we commonly know as fatigue, so that we require more or less regular periods of sleep to restore the body's vitality. During these periods of unconsciousness the brain functions at sharply reduced levels of energy while its 'batteries' are being recharged, so to speak. While the brain is resting, dreams may occur in which a sort of pseudo-reality is experienced by the self, operating in a fantasy-land of the mind's creation. Despite the universality of this phenomenon, its true nature is still far from being understood. During these periods of somnolence the mind is in abeyance but is nevertheless capable of responding quickly to emergency. Then, when the 'recharging' process is complete, consciousness floods back into a revitalized brain. Awareness returns, and the mind again seizes direct control of the body's mechanisms.

To acknowledge this necessary dependence of mind on body is to do no more, really, than to acknowledge the necessary dependence of *any* physical system on a source of energy and the ability of that physical system to respond. A blow to the head may cause unconsciousness, but a blow to my television set may also render *that* instrument inoperative. The fact that the physical instrument, the brain, through which consciousness is registered requires a proper upkeep of the body to keep it functioning is no more evidence of mind/brain *identity*, or of consciousness as *residing in* the brain, than it is of the television program I am watching as *residing in* my TV set. It seems obvious that the dualist hypothesis I am advocating is in no way jeopardized in either instance.

The mind is not simply a "category mistake", as Gilbert Ryle, author of *The Ghost in the Machine*, called it. Mind and consciousness are real, if immaterial, entities, no less than the values of love, truth, beauty, honesty, and friendship that we hold dear are real. Indeed, the mind is, if anything, *more* real than the material brain, because it is what enables us to *perceive* these values. We have to understand that the real is not just the material; this is reductionism's fundamental mistake. There is a real mental and spiritual realm, which I call the *noetic*, that *animates* the material world and gives it meaning. This noetic world does not 'emerge', like a ghost, from the material world—it is not composed of atoms or molecules—but it has primacy over it, as the creator has primacy over his creation. To perceive the world, and with it mind and consciousness, as 'nothing but' a collection of matter in motion is to perceive it from the most poverty-stricken of perspectives. Such a perspective restricts us forever to the role of engineers mired in the nuts and bolts of technology, of plumbers and electricians looking for the miracle of being in the electrochemical wiring of a physical system. Granted we need plumbers and electricians [we call them neurosurgeons] to occasionally repair the damaged electrochemical circuitry of the brain, but let no one mistake the map for the territory. The ontological reality of conscious mind is simply its *being*. A dualist perspective of both the mental and the physical realities of life accommodates the paradoxes between them by accepting the mental and the physical as *complementary* attributes of their expression.

A philosophy of dualism seems to accord, not only with Bohr's notions of complementarity but also with the quantum concept of a vast, inseparable, interconnected *wholeness* that physicists now increasingly feel best describes the physical nature of the universe at its most fundamental level. Some physicists, indeed, have gone further and have toyed with the idea that the universe *itself* may be conscious. Among them is Menas Kafatos, of George Mason University, who in *The Conscious Universe* written jointly with Robert Nadeau explores the notion that consciousness may be "embedded in the universe,"[122] a view that is clearly reminiscent of David Bohm's. The Kafatos view to some extent mirror's Spinoza's, the seventeenth century philosopher who thought that God was both *immanent* in nature and yet ontologically distinct, a concept that Einstein also favored. The flavor of Kafatos' thinking is best conveyed by the following quotation from his recent book:

"The cosmos is a dynamic sea of energy manifesting itself in entangled quanta which results in a seamless wholeness on the most primary level... What we mean by a conscious universe (is one that is) in accord with the totality of the (physical) facts and is anthropocentric only to the extent that it does answer to the very basic human need to feel that a profound spiritual awareness of unity with the whole cannot be deemed illusory from a scientific point of view." The universe "must be self-reflectively aware of itself as reality-in-itself to manifest the order that is the prior condition for all manifestations of being." The paradox is that "Scientific knowledge conditions us into an awareness of this whole and yet cannot fully affirm or 'prove' its existence in strictly scientific terms...the evidence for the existence of the ineffable and mysterious disclosed by modern physics is as near as the dance of particles that make up our bodies and as far as the furthest regions of the cosmos. The results of the experiments testing Bell's Theorem [the Aspect Experiments] suggest that all the parts, or any manifestation of 'being' in the vast cosmos, are seamlessly interconnected in the unity of

'Being'. Yet quantum physics also says that the ground of Being for all this being will never be subsumed by rational understanding."[123]

The reader will already be acquainted to some extent with Bohm's metaphysics. Bohm came to the conclusion that both matter and consciousness had some sort of "common ground", which was, in fact, the implicate order, that is, the immediate and primary actuality of being. Citing the work of Karl Pribram and others Bohm concludes—at least so far as memory is concerned—that information is not localized in any particular area of the brain but is so to speak "enfolded" over the entire brain structure, somewhat in the manner of the hologram. In the hologram, as has been indicated, the entire image of the viewed object is present in every section of the hologram; there is no one-to-one correspondence, as there is in a normal photograph, between parts of the actual illuminated object and parts of an image of this object on the holographic plate. Rather, the interference pattern of light which has produced the hologram is relevant to the entire illuminated object, and each region of the hologram is relevant to the whole of the interference pattern on the plate. There is a new notion of order here, Bohm notes, which is different from that of the classical Cartesian grid. "This order is not to be understood solely in terms of a regular arrangement of *events* (e.g. in a series)...(but) rather as a *total order* contained in some *implicit* sense in each region of space and time."[124]

I find it fascinating that both Bohm and Sperry have employed the same broadcasting analogy that I have found useful. Thus, Bohm writes:

> "In a television broadcast the visual image is translated into a time order, which is 'carried' by the radio wave...the radio wave carries the visual image in an implicate order...the function of the receiver is then to *explicate* this order, i.e. to 'unfold' it in the form of a new visual image... In all cases, the con-

tent or meaning that is 'enfolded' and 'carried' is primarily an order and a measure, permitting the development of a structure. With a radio wave this structure can be that of a verbal communication, a visual image, etc., but with the hologram far more subtle structures can be involved in this way... More generally, such order and measure can be 'enfolded' and 'carried' not only in electromagnetic waves... but also in sound...and in other countless forms of movement... To generalize, so as to emphasize undivided wholeness, we shall say that what 'carries' an implicate order is the *holomovement*, which is an unbroken and undivided totality... In certain cases we can abstract particular aspects of the holomovement (e.g. light, electrons, sound, etc.)...(but) in its totality the holomovement is not limited in any specifiable way at all...*the holomovement is undefined and immeasurable.*"

"Of course", Bohm goes on to explain, "consciousness is more than what has been described above... In listening to music, e.g., *one is directly perceiving an implicate order*...this order is *active* in the sense that it continually flows into emotional, physical, and other responses that are inseparable from the transformations from which it is essentially constituted."[125]

Bohm speaks of the process of enfoldment of the implicate order as being "bound by a force of overall necessity", in which the basic reality is not, as in current theories of relativistic physics, a point-event occurring in some small region of space and time, but rather "a *moment* which, like the moment of consciousness, cannot be precisely related to events in space and time...but is extended in space and has duration in time." It is Bohm's view that mind and matter are not separately existent but that "mind enfolds matter in general and therefore the body in particular...the more comprehensive, deeper, and more inward actuality is neither mind nor body but rather a yet higher-dimensional actuality, which is their common ground, and which is of a nature beyond both... In this higher-dimensional ground the implicate order prevails...within this ground *what is*, is movement, which is represented in thought as the co-presence of many phases of the implicate order...so that we do not say that mind and body causally affect each other, but rather that the movements of both are the outcome of related projections of a common higher-dimensional ground."

"The fundamental law, then, is of an immense multi-dimensional ground; and the projections from this ground determine whatever time-orders there may be... This we may call the ground of all that is."[126] Continuing, Bohm asks: "Is this ground the absolute end of everything?" Bohm does not appear willing to come right out and say. Rather, he postulates the possibility of an infinite regression, suggesting that "Through the force of an even deeper, more inward, necessity in this totality...'the totality of all that is'...there could, in principle, be an infinity of further development beyond it."[127]

Bohm's profundity notwithstanding, I find these thoughts of his concerning an infinite regression strangely unsatisfying, because they bespeak an unwillingness on his part to make the leap of faith they seem to call for. We need not anthropomorphize such a leap, but we need to feel that the immense ground to which Bohm refers is not simply a cold, impersonal reality. We need to feel that there is a purpose to it—a word that is oddly absent from Bohm's lexicon—and that man, as a manifestation of this purpose and this higher-dimensional ground, has a genuine home in the universe.

I am comforted by one very important observation, namely, that the new physics no longer forbids a science of the mind that is non-reductive. On the contrary, the new physics opens the way for a vision of reality in which mind and matter play complementary roles. In this new vision mind co-exists with matter in a dual relationship where mind is primary but where a material world is required for its expression. In this conception of the universe mind is neither subservient to nor emergent from matter but is, in fact, its creator. I am convinced that we have for too long been seduced by a philosophy of reductionism which turns the mind/body relationship upside down. It should always be remembered that mind is the primary reality which gives *meaning* to matter and that no investigative discipline which deliberately excludes mind and consciousness from the principles that govern the universe can be truly scientific. It may pay us to reflect deeply on Roger Penrose's comment that "It is only the phenomenon of consciousness that can conjure a putative 'theoretical' universe into actual existence."

A theory of dualism permits us to think of life and consciousness, not as existing apart from matter in some ethereal realm, but as existing in conjunction with matter when physical conditions are appropriate for their manifestation. *There is no compelling reason to suppose that matter is the only reality.* Indeed, there is abundant evidence to indicate that all the intangible mental and spiritual aspects of our lives constitute at least an equal, and perhaps more fundamental, reality. A theory of being based on a recognition of the complementary aspects of both realities has no difficulty in accepting the fact of consciousness and the fact of life as co-existent manifestations of a common ground, the ground of *all that is,* that is, of some final, ultimate Cause. We may call this ground God, or Brahman, or Allah, or even an *élan vital* à la Bergson. The point is simply that it is final and ultimate—there is no going beyond it for an explanation. In Rudolph Otto's phrase it is the "numinous" and "wholly other".[128] Language fails us in expressing this ultimate reality, forcing us to fall back on anthropomorphic religious images and icons which, in my opinion, only serve to demean the ineffable.

If we adopt a dualistic point of view, then life, mind, and consciousness are simply fundamental realities that co-exist with material substance in any universe it is possible for us to know. Life and consciousness, in this view, are not to be regarded as mysteriously emerging from some substrata of material substance but are to be understood as the *primary reality of that which is,* with matter the necessary medium for their expression. In other words, as Roger Sperry concluded, mind controls matter, not the other way around. This solves a lot of problems and is quite as 'scientific' as the materialist insistence that life is simply an "efflorescence" on a "dunghill of corruption" [Peter Atkins]. By postulating *first* the fact of life and consciousness as the universe's fundamental reality, we have a plausible explanation of the origin of those material conditions under which life is able to manifest itself, whereas the reverse—mind from matter and life from non-life—is impossible. In other words, I believe it makes a lot of sense to start from *the one reality we know best,* namely the existence of self, mind, and spirit, which constitute the noetic realm of our experience, and extrapolate backwards to matter, rather than to start with dumb matter and extrapolate forwards to life.

A universal field of consciousness animating our material brains is no more far-fetched, to my way of thinking, than universal gravitation. Science has not yet discovered such a universal field of consciousness, but neither has it discovered the means by which non-local quantum influences are instantaneously transmitted across millions of miles of 'empty' space. Consciousness, too, is real, 'though we know little of the mechanism by which it is manifested. Absence of evidence is not evidence of absence. It is not credible that consciousness can be 'nothing but' the jiggling of neurons in the cell walls of the Bose-Einstein condensate of the brain. It is not credible that consciousness can be simply an *emergent property* of the brain. As E.W.F. Tomlin has written in *The Approach to Metaphysics:*

> "It is one thing to prove that thought and the brain are intimately connected... It is quite another to assert...that the brain is the cause, or even the seat, of our thinking...for what does this theory imply? If the brain is the cause of our thinking—of *all* our thinking—then it is the cause, among other things, of the thought that this is so...and if this instrument and everything to do with it is material, there is no

sense in saying that one or other of its conditions is "true". A material thing just is. The distinction between truth and falsehood is in no way applicable to it. If, then, it is maintained that thought is the product of the brain, the whole edifice of philosophy collapses, and along with it—and this is a point of great importance—the whole of science."[129]

Tomlin's point is well taken. If thought is simply chemistry, or a pattern of electrical activity arising out of itself, if it is not the result of a purposeful self-awareness, of a conscious mental effort, why should any of its conclusions be trusted? Why should one pattern of electrical or chemical activity or jiggling of neurons in and of itself be superior to any other? What makes one self-induced pattern more correct than any other? It would seem that a self-catalyzing movement of molecules in the brain, without the supervision of an intelligent agency, could have no claim to truth, other than a purely accidental one, beyond that of any other similar self-catalyzing pattern. What Tomlin says is that thoughts or ideas cannot be *the same thing* as the brain; the brain is material, thoughts are immaterial. Thinking is teleological, that is, purposeful or truth-seeking. If thoughts were *identical* to certain brain states, this teleology would be physically embedded, somehow, in the brain's neuronal structure—but it is nowhere to be found there. Hence it must reside elsewhere, namely, in the mind, which is immaterial and distinct from the brain. Conclusion: Brain states cannot themselves be thoughts. Rather, *thoughts determine brain states*. This is the same conclusion Roger Sperry reached after decades of research into brain functioning.

Elsewhere in *The Approach to Metaphysics* Tomlin confirms my own feelings about the necessary mutual interdependence of mind and matter:

"Granted...that the essence of mind is to know, the inference is that matter (if it is the creator of mind) had every intention of putting its creature to some use. In other words, matter must have experienced a need to be known...so that, in creating mind, it satisfied at least this aspiration. Alternatively, if mind created matter, ...the inference is that it experienced the need to exercise its functions in ways that the presence of a world of objects best facilitated...whichever alternative is chosen...the relationship subsisting between mind and its object is a *necessary, intimate, and inevitable* one...[italics mine]. Any theory of knowledge which fails to account for at least some part of this necessity can hardly be classed as a theory of knowledge at all."[130]

This is the essence of my dualistic view of mind and matter, of brain and consciousness. It is that of a necessary, fundamental, and inseparable wholeness, as basic as that of wave and particle in the quantum realm. Consciousness, whatever else it may be, or on whatever else it may depend, is an independent ontological reality in its own right, existing apart from the brain, like the electromagnetic spectrum, but requiring a brain, or a nervous system of some sort, to make its reality manifest. The precise connection between mind and matter may remain forever unknowable—at least until science begins to acknowledge the existence of a noetic realm beyond matter. If science can acquiesce in the notion of non-locality, it ought to be able to accept the possibility of the existence of a noetic realm capable of directly affecting the motions of the atoms in our brains and bodies.

It seems self-evident to me that we live in a dualistic world, one in which mind reigns supreme over matter while nevertheless depending on the latter for its expression. I was overwhelmed last night by an experience that, for me, was clinching evidence of mind's supremacy. Through the medium of television I watched a performance of the First Tschaikowsky Piano Concerto by the brilliant young Russian pianist, Evgeny Kissin. I was captivated by the way in which mind was in control of the entire performance, as evidenced in the flying fingers of the virtuoso's hands as they glided masterfully over the keys and in the trance-like expression on the orchestra conductor's face as he skillfully transmitted every nuance of the music to the instrumentalists. The exquisite harmony of the operation was something to behold. Mind was in absolute control every step of the way. Mind directed the brain which moved the muscles of the body to play the perfectly executed notes on the musical instruments. Mind directed the encoding of both sight and sound onto an invisible electronic signal and then sent this signal out over the airwaves. Mind directed the construction and operation of the receiving instrument, the television set, which reconstituted the signal into a faithful reproduction of the original performance as the signal was plucked from a mysterious electromagnetic medium that surrounded it. Lastly, then, mind somehow equally mysteriously transformed the waves of sight and sound impinging on the viewer's eyes and ears from the electronic instrument he was watching into a mental and emotional sensation in the brain that I can only describe as transcendent. This emotional sensation was a spiritual experience which carried its own ontological credentials. It was by no stretch of the imagination identical to a jiggling of the neuron cell walls in the Bose-Einstein condensate of the brain.

None of this, I submit, can be reconciled with the notion of a universe in which matter is the only reality. Nor can it be reconciled with a universe in which mind is emergent from matter, for then matter would be the creator, the artist, rather than, as we have seen, the other way around. Mind, I am convinced, is what directs and controls matter. There is an ontological distinction between the two which Roger Sperry was persuaded was unique and fundamental. Mind and matter, I believe, are two fundamental aspects of a dualism that pervades the universe. In my penultimate chapter I want to explore how the undeniable facts of our awareness of mind and consciousness relate to two other mysterious aspects of the physical universe, namely, to our notions of time and entropy. It will be seen, I think, that these also partake of a noetic realm and possess a dual nature as inscrutable as anything we have examined heretofore.

EIGHTEEN

OF TIME AND ENTROPY

"The universe is simmering down, like a giant stew left to cook
for four billion years; sooner or later we won't be able
to tell the carrots from the onions."
–*Arthur Bloch*

The joker who remarked that time was nature's way of keeping everything from happening all at once may not, it turns out, have been so far off the mark. If everything *did* happen at once there would be no past or future—just a constant sense of universal 'now'. What is it, then, that makes time seem to pass, or to flow? It is, plainly, a quality of time that is called *duration*, which has a counterpart in the quality of space called *extension*. Objects have extension (dimension) in space and they also have duration in time. If physical objects did not possess both of these attributes, we could only talk about dimensionless points in space 'existing' in zero time. Such a concept is obviously meaningless and gives rise to paradoxes such as those of Zeno, who tried to show through them that motion was impossible. If motion is an illusion, then time must be an illusion, also. We know from experience, however, that motion is decidedly real, and it follows, therefore, that we must also embrace time as a reality, at least in its aspect of duration, which, by the laws of physics, measures the elapsed time required for a material object to go from point "A" to point "B". Both time and motion are firmly anchored in the Einsteinian relativity relationships that govern the universe.

But to embrace time and motion as fundamental physical, or at least perceptive, realities says little about their ultimate nature. If the essence of time is duration, what is it that endures? What endures is *being*, and the essence of that endurance is *becoming*. Newton notwithstanding, there is no absolute time in the universe which "flows equably without relation to anything external". From this it follows that there is also no object which is at absolute rest, for to be at absolute rest means that there is no motion, no duration, and hence no becoming. A body which is absolutely at rest with respect to everything else in the universe literally does not exist.

The inescapable conclusion is that everything in the universe is in some kind of motion, in some state of becoming, so that everything which exists has duration. In their book, *The Arrow of Time*, Peter Coveney and Roger Highfield point out that:

> "There is no absolute state of rest, lacking motion...it all depends on one's frame of reference. Consider the simplest example, a universe cleared of everything except two balls. If the distance between the two balls is steadily increasing, it is impossible to say whether one, or the other, or both are moving. It is impossible to assign a privileged status to any single such frame of reference."[131]

Let us ponder the implications. If it is indeed the case that nothing exists which is at absolute rest, and that becoming necessarily implies duration, then time is not something which begins and ends—it is continuous. That is essentially why Zeno's paradox fails; time is continuous and cannot be stopped by repeated subdivision. Achilles manages to catch, and to overtake, the tortoise because motion (becoming) is the fundamental reality. And because not even light is instantaneous, all motion has *duration*. As long as Achilles does not break a leg, he is bound to overtake the tortoise because his motion and forward progress are quite independent of any measurement of duration. The chain of causality runs from motion to duration and not the other way around.

What this implies further, I think, is that pure *being*, in the Platonic sense, is an illusion; there is only being in the process of *becoming*. The modern philosopher, Alfred North Whitehead, was a strong supporter of the idea that the universe is not static but is always in process of becoming. Change, not stasis, is the fundamental reality. This, as we have seen, is also the view toward which modern physics is heading, as expressed in the science and philosophy of David Bohm. The notion of duration is inextricably interwoven with the continual process of becoming. There is no use asking if anything existed before the Big Bang because this presupposes a beginning and an end to time. It is my belief that there has *always* been 'something' rather than 'nothing'. Even the vacuum has a certain permanence and, indeed, is thought to contain immense energy and structure. The underlying reality of the universe, I believe, is one of flux and change in an eternal process of *becoming*. In this reality, as in the concept of a circle, time has no beginning and no end but has infinite duration.

Consider the alternative. If time is not continuous, then we must postulate an instant of zero time, of no duration, which is a logical contradiction. An instant of zero time is like a mathematical point of no extension. Neither can ever achieve reality because there is an unbridgeable discontinuity between being and not-being, between 'something' and 'nothing'. A mathematical point has no real existence because it is always possible to insert another point between any two loci on a line no matter how proximate they may be. One can get from a dimensionless point to the concept of a line only by a leap of faith, a leap which—fortunately—is vouchsafed to us via everyday experience. In the same way, one can get from the concept of zero time to duration only by another leap of faith, namely, the faith that time is, in fact, unending. There is really no other conclusion.

If we recognize duration as a necessary and complementary aspect to spatial extension, then we comprehend Einstein's description of the universe as a space-time *continuum*. There are truly four dimensions to the universe, three of space and one of time. The locus of any point in space is meaningless without also an accompanying determination of time. But it is precisely here that we run into complexity, because, just as there exists no unique reference frame for motion, so there exists no unique reference frame for time. Time and motion are, in this sense, observer-dependent.

What I mean by this is that all events in the universe are essentially *local;* we see all time and motion from a strictly local perspective. The fundamental reason for this, as I have already explained, is that the speed of light is finite, so that information does not reach all observers instantaneously. When we look out at the stars, we see them, not as they are 'now', meaning in our time, but as they were millions of years ago, because it has taken that long for their light to reach us. For all we know, the universe beyond our solar system may have already vanished, because it takes light from the nearest star, *Alpha Centauri*, 4.4 years to reach us. We are, therefore, never aware of how things are 'now', at this instant, because there *is* no universal instant. A universal 'now' exists only if information about all events in the universe can be communicated to all observers instantaneously. A universal 'now' is conceivable only in the context of a universal consciousness.

The finite speed of light [300,000 kms/sec] is the main reason why our experience of events in the universe is what I call *local*. However, the matter is more complex than that. Our experience of time is also affected by the velocity with which we are moving as well as by the intensity of the gravitational field in which we happen to find ourselves. For example, if we were to accelerate away from Earth at near light speed or we were to find ourselves in the intense gravitational field of a black hole[132], we would—in addition to encountering normal time-delay—experience a phenomenon known as *time dilation*. What this means is that, *as locally experienced*, time actually slows down as we measure it. Both our clocks and our biological rhythms would run more slowly, so that we would actually *age* more slowly than the friend we had left at home on Earth. If you find this difficult to believe, consider that this phenomenon, referred to as the *Twins Paradox*, has actually been observed, scientifically, on many occasions, from the increased longevity of accelerated sub-atomic particles in a cyclotron to the minute time discrepancies registered by highly precise atomic clocks that have been flown in opposite directions around the world. Time can actually be stretched or dilated under these conditions. It is a curious fact that a second, as measured on Earth, is not a constant unit of time throughout the universe. If, someday, we develop the technology, it will be possible to send a human being on an interstellar trip and return him to Earth hundreds or even thousands of years in the future!

All of this follows from standard relativity theory, and it holds not only for time, but for physical extension as well. A yardstick, for example, that is accelerated to near the speed of light will shrink and its mass will become almost infinitely great. That is why, fundamentally, nothing can travel faster than light. At near-light speed mass and inertia increase exponentially, so that no conceivable force can accelerate a material object any further.

These are mysteries of time and motion that defy common experience and, perhaps, even common sense. Yet there is no doubt in the minds of physicists that these relativistic effects are real and that they would be experienced more generally by humans if everything on Earth did not move so slowly—slowly, that is, relative to the speed of light! There are other mysteries, as well. It is common human experience that time has *direction* in addition to *duration*, namely, that time has an 'arrow' which points from 'past' to 'future'. Yet, surprisingly, neither classical physics, nor relativity theory, nor quantum mechanics explicitly recognizes any 'arrow'. Throughout physics, except in the branch known as thermodynamics, exchanges of energy between particles are considered to be time-symmetric, in other words, reversible. The concept of a direction to time, in the sense of past, present, and future, is fairly recent and is found only in a branch of physics called *irreversible thermodynamics*.

189

Thermodynamics, as a specific discipline within physics, dates only from about the middle of the nineteenth century. This was an era when the steam engine was coming into its own and when a number of engineers and physicists were interested in increasing its efficiency, for it was recognized at an early date that no steam engine was 100% efficient. That is, some of the heat energy produced by a steam engine was lost to its surroundings, in other words, it was dissipated. This meant that, although work and heat were equivalent, dissipation created a fundamental assymetry, so that while work could be transformed 100% into heat, the opposite was not possible. It was Rudolph Clausius, German pioneer researcher of the *Second Law of Thermodynamics*, who recognized that this heat loss gave a specific direction to time, which was irreversible. This notion he later sharpened, in 1865, into a concept called *entropy*.[133]

Entropy can be broadly defined as a measure of molecular randomness, and what the Second Law of Thermodynamics says is that entropy *always tends to increase* in isolated, far-from-equilibrium systems. Such systems, in which the entire universe must be included, tend constantly to run down, to dissipate energy, to disperse heat, so that molecular motion tends to become more and more disordered. When the disorder has reached an extreme, the entropy of the system is a maximum, and no further dispersion of energy is possible. All semblance of macroscopic order and structure vanishes. As applied to the cosmos itself, the Second Law forecasts that the universe will continue to run down, like a clock, and will ultimately reach a state of maximum entropy known as the "heat death", a phrase popularized by Arthur Eddington. Eddington was so impressed by the Second Law and the concept of entropy that he once wrote to an inquirer:

> "The law that entropy always increases—the Second Law of Thermodynamics—holds, I think, the supreme position among the laws of nature. If someone points out to you that your pet theory of the universe is in disagreement with Maxwell's

equations—then so much the worse for Maxwell's equations. If it is found to be contradicted by observation, well, these experimentalists do bungle things sometimes. But if your theory is found to be against the Second Law of Thermodynamics, I can give you no hope; there is nothing for it but to collapse in deepest humiliation."[134]

Is the inexorability of the Second Law, in fact, our destiny? Scientists, as well as philosophers, are undecided. There is an imaginative quotation from Asimov's *Last Question* which is cited by Ilya Prigogine, winner of the 1977 Nobel Prize for chemistry, in his introduction to Coveney and Highfield's recent book, *The Arrow of Time*. In this citation a dying civilization keeps asking a giant computer:

"Will we some day be able to overcome the Second Law of Thermodynamics?", and the computer answers, 'The data are insufficient.' Billions of years pass by, stars and galaxies die, while the computer, directly connected to spacetime, continues to collect data. Finally, there is no information left to be gathered any longer, nothing 'exists' any more, but the computer goes on computing and discovering correlations. Finally it reaches the answer. There is no longer anyone there to learn, but the computer now knows how to overcome the Second Law. *And there was Light...*"[135]

Cosmologists are of varying opinions regarding the Second Law, but most of them agree that the universe *is* running down, which implies that it was, at some earlier date in its history, so to speak, 'wound up'. How this winding-up process occurred, and when, is in dispute, but Roger Penrose, one of the most eminent of the clan, thinks it occurred at the very beginning. "For some reason," Penrose writes in *The Emperor's New Mind*, "the universe was created in a very special (low entropy) state...the Second Law demands that, in its initial state, the entropy of the universe was at some sort of *minimum*, not a maximum!" In fact, affirms Penrose, it appears that the universe at its creation was "precisely organized" to a degree that is literally incomprehensible to the human mind. The number Penrose comes up with is a factor of one part in $10^{10^{123}}$, a number so humongous that "one could not possibly even write the number down in the ordinary denary notation: it would be one followed by 10^{123} successive zeroes..."

"The precision needed to set the universe on its course is seen to be in no way inferior to that extraordinary precision that we have already become accustomed to in the superb dynamical equations (Newton's, Maxwell's, Einstein's) which govern the behaviour of things from moment to moment."[136]

What will happen if there should be, as is predicted by some theories, a *Big Crunch* at some time in the future following the initial *Big Bang?* If, in the future, the universe's present expansion ends, and it starts to collapse, some cosmologists have contended that entropy will reverse and that time will run backward, but Penrose is unpersuaded of this. He argues that entropy will go on rising, as it now seems to be doing in Black Holes, which are small-scale versions of the 'Big Crunch' among certain stars whose gravitation is collapsing. Penrose points out that the nature of the singularity at the universe's creation [Big Bang theory] was probably very different from the nature of the singularity that is presupposed at its final collapse, should this occur. The entropy at final collapse will be a maximum, if the Second Law continues to operate, while the entropy of the initial singularity was extraordinarily low, owing to a constraint known as the Weyl Curvature. These are technical, even speculative, conclusions on which I am not qualified to comment, but they suggest that the Second Law *can*, indeed, be overcome should a new universe, following an endless cycle of death and rebirth, emerge from the old.

A 'Big Crunch' in the universe's future is, in any event, not a foregone conclusion. The universe may simply go on expanding, or it may reach a point of maximum expansion and then tremble forever, like a dewdrop on a petal, between the two possibilities of infinite expansion or contraction. We simply do not know, because it has not proved possible, so far, to accurately compute all the matter in the universe. Beyond a certain point—the Omega Point—too little matter leads to infinite expansion, too much to ultimate contraction. The universe, at present, seems approximately balanced between the two extremes.

In the universe we inhabit, the irreversibility of the Second Law is what gives direction to time, it is what determines time's *arrow*. Everyday evidence of this irreversibility is seen in the fact that smashed teacups do not reassemble themselves, that fruit decays, and that living organisms grow old and die. There is another way, however, to understand the inevitability of the Second Law. The Second Law can be given a statistical interpretation which rests on the fact that, simply from the standpoint of probability, there are many more *opportunities* for any organized system to fall into disorder than to maintain a specified complexity. The maintenance of *specified order* implies a *directed* input of energy from outside the system, because an isolated system cannot organize itself, the proponents of "self-catalysis" notwithstanding. An isolated system, because it must obey the Second Law, cannot lower its own entropy.

For a system to be able to lower its own entropy it must not only receive an input of raw energy from 'outside', but the input of that energy must be somehow directed in an intelligent manner. Quite bluntly, it must be purposefully directed. A whirlwind blowing over a junkyard will not assemble a 747 airplane. Order thus implies the *intelligent* direction of raw energy, not simply its availability. In the cosmos it implies that something 'wound up' the system at its beginning according to very precise laws and principles which guided its subsequent evolution. In the human being, indeed in every living organism, it implies a morphology, that is, the existence of laws of form and structure, which guide the development of the embryo through all of its stages of development. An appeal to the Darwinian principle of *natural selection* simply will not do. All that this principle has ever been able to explain is that

"that which survives, survives". It has been a catch-all for a wide variety of miscellaneous factors that together contribute to an organism's 'success'. The strong implication of the existence of laws of form and structure is that there exists a powerful creative force, a teleology if you will, that has not only provided the raw energy required to assemble the universe but has given it intelligent and purposeful direction. The *Argument from Design* is one of the strongest arguments that have been made in support of Deity. Whether it appeals to you or not, it is in any case next to impossible, as Penrose and others have pointed out, that a highly specific complexity at the creation could have been the result of pure 'chance'.

Penrose writes:

> "We ourselves are configurations of ridiculously tiny entropy! ... High entropy states are, in a sense, the 'natural' states, which do not need further explanation. But the low entropy states in the past are a puzzle... We should not be surprised if, *given* a low entropy state, the entropy turns out to be higher at a later time... What *should* surprise us is that entropy gets more ridiculously tiny the farther and farther that we examine it in the past... There was indeed something constraining the system in the past...something *forced* the entropy to be low..."[137]

Penrose does not suggest what this "something" might have been, but we may draw our own conclusions. That same "something", I believe, is clearly operative in the emergence of highly ordered far-from-equilibrium systems, such as ourselves, in a universe that has been running down for ten billion years and in which complex low entropy life forms, so far as Earth is concerned, have only just emerged in the most recent period of its evolution.

This digression into entropy and origins has taken me a little far afield, but an understanding of entropy is clearly important to appreciating the nature of time. The organized and specified complexity of living systems needs to be explained, in the face of the Second Law, as something other than the operation of blind chance and of "survival of the fittest". Time and entropy together are aspects of the material universe which are necessary concomitants of its physical structure and being. Both are reflections of the exquisite Intelligence which sustains and directs life, mind, and consciousness.

How can the phenomenon of entropy and our awareness of time's duration be squared with the newly-discovered reality of non-locality, of instantaneous non-local universal connections? [See Appendix "B"]

Non-locality, in the present state of our understanding of physics, is one of the impenetrable mysteries. To my way of thinking non-locality is simply another piece of evidence that the odds which Roger Penrose has placed on the chance creation of the cosmos, namely, one chance in ten to the 123rd power of ten (!!) are, if anything, too generous. As I have indicated, non-locality is perhaps best understood, not as a phenomenon of communication in a space-time continuum, but as a *built-in* feature of that continuum. It would not be helpful to encumber this newly-discovered reality with too much metaphysical baggage, yet I find the fact of its reality reassuring. It somehow leapfrogs the concepts of space-time-duration in a way which suggests that almost anything is possible. It gives our intimations of immortality a real metaphysical jolt! The universe, and our places in it, are obviously realities far more wondrous than we could ever have imagined. The proven existence of instantaneous non-local connections throughout the universe, defying time and entropy, seems to loosen the chains on our earthly existence by titillating us with a future of unlimited possibilities.

Finally, there is another aspect to time—the psychological— which cannot be scientifically defined or measured and is clearly not the same for everyone. The value of a human life, for example, is always ultimately scored in terms of what we have done and how well we have done it. The fact that the human lifespan is limited is what renders it poignant and meaningful. The psychological value of time may therefore, from our perspective, be its most important element. If there is a purpose to our presence on Earth, it cannot be simply longevity or well-being but it must be something more, namely, the lessons that are to be learned from it. Those lessons and how we apply them constitute our *karma* throughout eternity. In this scheme of things the temporal passage of events plays only a minor role, albeit a necessary one, for it is only in the human experiencing of time's flow and its duration in a physical space-time environment that those lessons can be learned.

NINETEEN

A SUMMING-UP

"The new way of seeing things will involve an imaginative leap that will astonish us. In any case, it seems that the quantum mechanical description will be superseded. In this it is like all theories made by man. But to an unusual extent its ultimate fate is apparent in its internal structure. It carries in itself the seeds of its own destruction."
–John Stewart Bell

"I am afraid of this word, reality."
–Arthur Eddington

In the foregoing chapters I have led you through a good deal of modern physics, as well as some metaphysics, in an effort to come to grips with the most fundamental questions we can pose, namely, who we are, why we are here, and where we may be going. From my perspective a good deal has been learned, but what impresses me just as much, if not more, is how much about the universe is still unlearned, and can probably never be learned, because the mystery of what lies 'out there' is in a kind of infinite regress. Dreams of a 'final' theory are just that—dreams. We can be grateful to Kurt Gödel for that revelation, if to no one else.

I have been asked, "Why physics?", and my answer has been that physics is the science of the physical, of the material world which is most immediate to our experience. Is it not, perhaps, logical to begin with an analysis of that world, which has traditionally been looked to for an explanation of why things are the way they are, particularly during the last few hundred years since the widespread adoption of the scientific method? We have had enough of armchair philosophers. Physics appealed to me as a rational, systematic, and *scientific* way to approach the subject.

Alas, if I may be allowed to misquote Euclid, there is no royal road to truth, and the exercise I have been through has demonstrated to me the very real limitations of the scientific method. Science is only one of our avenues to truth, and it will never be able to tell us everything that we would like to know about ourselves. Roger Penrose has written: "It is my opinion that our present picture of physical reality, particularly in relation to the nature of *time*, is due for a grand shake-up—even greater, perhaps, than that which has already been provided by present-day relativity and quantum mechanics."[138] This thought has been echoed by a number of physicists, but I doubt that such a "shake-up", when it comes, will bring us much closer to 'ultimate' truth unless it includes also a metaphysics of the mind.

For the mind, until recently, has been systematically excluded from scientific study. What has been systematically studied is the brain, but despite the intensity and depth of research, no semblance of *mind* has been found there. Reductionism is still the rage in biology. Some scientists, as well as some philosophers, nevertheless, have always recognized that mind and brain *cannot* be identical. I have argued—I hope with some persuasion—that there is a fundamental dichotomy between the material and the mental that can best be understood in terms of a Cartesian dualism, encompassing the quantum mechanical notion of *complementarity*, of the logical necessity of the existence of opposites in a world of change and becoming, and of the basic primacy of the mental and the spiritual—the noetic—in all relationships. This is, admittedly, a metaphysical persuasion that I cannot 'prove' scientifically, but science, strictly speaking, cannot *prove* anything. It can only formulate theories and then, repeatedly, test them against the evidence.

There has been a major shift of scientific perspectives during the twentieth century, and as the twenty-first approaches that perspective is again changing. Scientists are increasingly aware of the fact that there is a world of reality beyond physics, a world of metaphysics, and that this world must be accorded at least the same recognition as the microcosmos which physicists have been diligently probing for a clue to truth. Nothing in physics has been so suggestive of the existence of this world as Bell's Theorem and the Aspect experiments that have supported it. The new physical concept of non-locality and all that it implies is the fourth leg on a stool—the other three being relativity, quantum mechanics, and complementarity—that may enable physicists to have a look at this new world from a new perspective superior to any they have had available to them heretofore.

This world of reality beyond science—the noetic realm—is to many thoughtful individuals, as it has been for centuries, the *only* world we can actually 'know'; all the rest is "pointer readings". My view of things, as the reader is by now abundantly aware, is that a dualistic perspective best embraces *both* realities, the material and the noetic, in a necessary reciprocity of action and re-action. The two worlds are, in a sense, a reflection of Newton's Third Law.[139] My 'gut' feeling—call it religious, if you will—is that there is a higher-dimensional reality beyond the noetic realm from which both the mental and the material emanate, and that this higher-dimensional reality or ground is what we have always called God. I do not wish to anthropomorphize the concept, but simply want to note that its characteristics reach beyond the merely mental to encompass the spiritual and the religious. While the mental/physical duality is witnessed in the life of all animals, the spiritual dimension appears restricted to man alone. The spiritual dimension is a reality that is different not only in degree but in kind from the merely mental.

Probably the greatest scientific genius of the century, Albert Einstein, once wrote: "Science without religion is lame; religion without science is blind."[140] Einstein was a physicist in awe of what he called "cosmic religious feeling." This feeling, he was careful to point out, does not involve any anthropomorphic conception of God. It "knows no dogma, no God conceived in man's image, ...(and) no church whose central teachings are based on it." Einstein maintained that "Cosmic religious feeling is the strongest and noblest motive for scientific research..." Historically, it may be noted, it has been at the basis of the scientist's tradition- al faith in the rationality of the universe and therefore also in the value of scientific research.

I am in accord with Penrose, Baggott, and others who think that a more profound understanding of the nature of time is need- ed in order to make further substantial progress in science. For such concepts as *being, becoming,* and *continuity*—the basic stuff of both physics and philosophy—are inextricably entangled with notions of time in some still mysterious fashion. The mystery goes back, as I have shown, to the paradoxes of Zeno, paradoxes which continue to exert their fascination because rational thought is congenitally indisposed to accepting a discontinuity. Yet, when it suits their purposes, scientists have been quite willing to posit dis- continuities such as the Big Bang, quantum 'jumps', and even non-locality. "I accept the universe", declared early American author and critic, Margaret Fuller, to which Thomas Carlyle replied, "By God, she'd better!" It seems to me that, in adopting a philosophy of dualism, we, too, can "accept the universe" without having to force every scientific observation onto a Procrustean bed of reductionism.

There is a theory popular among certain cosmologists that the universe is "the ultimate free lunch", meaning that we don't need to look to any source or power beyond the universe in order to explain it. This theory argues that the universe has simply "orga- nized" itself into existence from a vacuum fluctuation and has then, in apparent violation of the Second Law of Thermodynamics, "self-catalyzed" the amazing variety of life forms, including ourselves, that we see all about us and which give it meaning. There is even a theory, attributable to John Wheeler, that the universe is an immense "delayed choice experi- ment" by which we, as observers looking backward through time and space, may be said to be responsible for our own creation!

My opinion of such speculations is that they bespeak an intel- lectual outlook on the part of their protagonists that is totally devoid of any "cosmic religious feeling". It is, of course, possible to approach both science and philosophy from this perspective, but then what is the point? If we exclude the ineffable from our considerations and regard the universe as self-organizing, we are back to mindless mechanism, a universe without cause or purpose. Such an approach is, in my view, not only arrogant but metaphysically barren. It is the worst kind of reductionism, for it rejects *prima facie* any possibility that the universe, and man, may have a higher destiny.

It appears to me that, precisely because the universe is so fantastically complex, a great deal of humility is called for. If our experience of life in this universe teaches us anything, it should be that science does not have all the answers and that the power of man's intellect is limited. A measure of faith is needed irrespective of the conclusions one reaches, whether scientific or otherwise. All that science can do, in helping us to reach conclusions, is to organize the evidence available and to sharpen our minds and intellects. Science cannot—and has never pretended to—serve up revealed truth.

We have come back, via some kind of grand and strange loop, to the beginning of our inquiry into the nature of reality. I do not think that it has been wrong to begin with physics, because a knowledge of what scientists have learned about the material world can only prove helpful in widening our perspectives. But physics can deal only with the "how", never the "why", of any question, and it is the latter which interests us most. As Stanley L. Jaki, a Hungarian priest with doctorates in both theology *and* physics, has written: "True metaphysics implies a series of assertions about a Reality beyond the universe, as the cause of the reality of the universe itself."[141] Jaki quotes the following passage from C.S. Lewis to support his contention that the meaning of man resides in the universe itself:

> "Either there is significance in the whole process of things as well as in human activity, or there is no significance in human activity itself. It is an idle dream, at once cowardly and arrogant, that we can with-

draw the human soul, as a mere epiphenomenon, from a universe of idiotic force and yet hope, after that, to find for her some *faubourg* where she can keep a mock court in exile. You cannot have it both ways. If the world is meaningless, then so are we; if we mean something, we do not mean it alone..."[142]

I think it is very difficult for us, as individuals, to find a meaning in the universe for ourselves alone. I find the meaning of the universe in the reality of my relationship to those I love. That reality, for me, is timeless and somehow interwoven with my own reality in a strange and wonderful way that I do not profess to understand, but which I am convinced is profound. We must, in the last analysis, take what is given; we have no other choice. I believe that science can help us to comprehend somewhat more clearly that which is given, and how vast and wonderful it is, but no amount of *Grübelei* can clarify that meaning for us. In the end it must remain a personal meaning, different for each individual and yet ultimately the same. We must recognize that, but for an "accident of time" [Hesse], 'I' might have been 'you' and that our roles might have been reversed. That should be enough to keep even the most arrogant of us humble.

What the wider meaning of the universe may be—the universe that exists 'out there' in the immense intergalactic reaches of space—no human being can fathom. It seems clear that C.S. Lewis's conclusion is unchallengeable: *Either there is a purpose to the universe or we ourselves become meaningless.* Since the latter proposition is one that I must reject as tantamount to nihilism, I must also believe that the universe has a wider purpose. Now purpose, as I have already made clear, is a word with connotations of intelligence; an undirected purpose is an oxymoron. It follows that some sort of intelligence or mind directing the universe is a logical conclusion of the order we find in it. Only a supreme mind or consciousness directing the universe could give it the meaning it must have if we ourselves are not an irrelevant epiphenomenon in it, a mere "accident of time" with neither meaning nor purpose.

The comedian Woody Allen once quipped, "I'm not afraid to die—I just don't want to be there when it happens." That is, humorously put, the essence of our personal dilemma. All of our experience of the world, all the 'reality' we can ever know, is funneled through the personal 'I'. This reality is suspended for us eight hours each night, and we do not agonize over the fact that, during this period of unconsciousness, the rest of the world is passing us by. We are also not overly upset by the knowledge that a lot of history "passed us by" before we were born, but we are pained at the thought of leaving. What distresses us most, of course, is the thought of having to leave our loved ones behind, especially the thought that we may never see them again.

But we don't know this for a fact. What we know for a fact is that the material body disintegrates and is no more. Most of us, however, are not in love with our material bodies and, if we could have our druthers, we would gladly trade ours in for another. But our material bodies are not *us!* We left a lot of bodies behind as we were growing up, because our bodies have changed constantly over the years. We do not even have the same body we had a few years ago, because our bodies are constantly renewing themselves through the food we eat, the liquids we drink, the air we breathe, and the sunlight we absorb. Our physical bodies are literally changing throughout our lifetimes. Throughout these metamorphoses, however, we are convinced that we remain the same person. We are reminded of the Greek conundrum of the wooden sailing ship, which is replaced, plank by plank, over time, while sailing under the same name, flag, and crew. Is it the same ship, or a different ship, from the one that existed before? We are convinced we are the same person through time, because the ego does not change and neither our minds nor our memories have been erased. If there is, in fact, this real ontological distinction between our selves and our bodies, then the destruction of the material body can make no essential difference.

The paradox of spiritual continuity in a changing material body is strangely reminiscent of Zeno's paradox of motion. Zeno thought that by bringing time to a stop he could also halt motion, but in fact neither time nor motion can be stopped, since the reality is that both are *continuous*. In somewhat the same way the self, if it is real, must also be continuous. If it were technically feasible, all the atoms of my body could be substituted for all of yours, but I do not believe this would affect the essence of our souls by a single iota. What this suggests is that the essence of what we are is something non-material, as the great religions have always maintained. The essence of our being is not affected by the deconstruction of the body into its smallest constituent parts. Quantum theory has taught us that the parts derive their significance and *literally their very properties* from the character and nature of the whole. We—our spiritual selves—are the wholes from which our bodies derive any significance they may possess.

When the atheist philosopher, Sidney Hook, was once asked what he would say if he unexpectedly found himself in God's presence, his reply was, "Lord, you didn't give me enough evidence." That is the crux of our dilemma. There will never, ever, be enough 'evidence'. But the same thing might be said of some of our most cherished scientific theories, where new evidence is continually turning up, causing even established theories to be modified or radically altered to accommodate the newly-discovered facts. The history of physics in the last two hundred years is replete with modified or discarded theories that were once regarded as correct. We do not stop doing physics for lack of evidence. Science is as much a matter of faith as religion, but it is a poorer faith, I think, because it has until recently left man completely out of the picture. If, in the fullness of your understanding of what the limitations of science are, you arrive at the conclusion that there is a power in the universe which supersedes matter, there is no one in the parthenon of science who can gainsay you. For science does not deny "cosmic religious feeling", it simply regards it as *ultra vires*. We are perfectly free to accept another view of reality than the so-called scientific because, as noted, science itself has shifted its perspectives repeatedly. One can take a teleological view of the universe, or one can take one's science "straight", but one cannot take metaphysics out of it. Metaphysics is as integral a part of science as it is of religion; it is simply a matter of the kind of metaphysics one prefers.

Jim Baggott writes:

> "Despite the positivists' efforts to eradicate metaphysics from philosophy, the old metaphysical questions escaped virtually unscathed. I find it rather fascinating to observe that although the possibility of the existence of God and the relationship between mind and body no longer form part of the staple diet of the modern philosopher of science, they have become increasingly relevant to discussions on modern quantum physics. Three centuries of gloriously successful physics have brought us right back to the kind of speculation that it took three centuries of philosophy to reject as meaningless."[143]

"And what of God?", continues Baggott, "Does quantum theory provide any support for the idea that God is behind it all?" Baggott's surprising answer: "The God-hypothesis has many things to commend it...", but he concedes that there is no compelling reason at present for preferring this interpretation of quantum theory over any other. What he offers instead is the possibility of accepting the idea of *God without religion*. By this he means accepting the idea of God without all the formalized, ritualistic trappings of an organized church, with its blind, dogmatic insistence on certain 'truths'.

> "Once we accept God without religion, we can ask ourselves the all-important questions with something approaching intellectual rigour. The fact that we have lost the habit or the need to invoke the existence of God *should not prevent us from examining this possibility as a serious alternative to the interpretations of quantum theory discussed previ-*

*ously. It is, after all, no less metaphysical or bizarre
than some of the other possibilities we have considered so far."* [italics mine][144]

To this I can only say "Amen", for whatever the reality of our
relationship to God, it is surely not reducible to the simplistic
notions of reward and punishment that motivate so many of those
who regularly attend Sunday services. Nor does that relationship,
in my opinion, require the mediation of a professional caste of
priests. The true nature of our relationship to the eternal ground
is rather one that each of us, in the privacy of the inner sanctum
of the soul, must discern for himself.

The great Albert Einstein put it this way:

"The most beautiful and most profound emotion
we can experience is the sensation of the mystical.
It is the sower of all true science. He to whom this
emotion is a stranger, who can no longer wonder
and stand rapt in awe, is as good as dead. To know
that what is impenetrable to us really exists, manifesting itself to us as the highest wisdom and the
most radiant beauty which our dull faculties can
comprehend only in their most primitive forms—
this knowledge, this feeling, is at the center of true
religiousness."[145]

There is a very simple, yet beautiful, phrase which Christ
spoke to the apostles after the Resurrection. It is the message: *"Be
not afraid!"* This simple message captures the essence of what
these peregrinations have taught me, namely, that the religious
feelings of awe and wonder that man has experienced from his
earliest beginnings are not just some grand illusion but correspond to a profound reality. That reality, I think, is most keenly
felt in the unity of one soul with another when both recognize
themselves to *be* the other somewhat differently expressed. There
is no greater strength in the universe than the bond of love which

flows from such mutual recognition. With the accumulation of wisdom grows also the realization that there are many such reflections of ourselves in the world, if we could but know them. For the world cannot have been made for us alone; it must have been made for all of us as embodiments of a universal spirit which is self-consciously aware and which represents the idealization of the self in each of us. The most important conclusion, I feel, is that we are not alone, drifting aimlessly in a meaningless and accidental universe but are the purposeful products of Creation. We, ourselves, are the best evidence of the existence of a Supreme Intelligence, because there is no possibility, as I have tried to show, that the power of mind and consciousness could have come to us from any other source. A universe without man is almost inconceivable as a reflection of this Supreme Intelligence.

There is a famous 'proof' for God's existence that Gottfried Leibnitz cited some three hundred years ago in his *Philosophical Writings*. It goes like this:

> "The world cannot just *happen* to exist, and whatever (or whoever) caused it to exist must also exist, since the principle of sufficient reason means that something cannot come from nothing: *Ex nihilo, nihilo fit*. Furthermore, the ultimate, or first, cause of the world must exist outside the world. God is the only sufficient reason for the existence of the world. The world exists, therefore it is necessary for God also to exist."[146]

This 'proof' has in it the element of dualism which I find fundamental to everything that is. One can quarrel with it, but one can also accept it as reasonable. In the last analysis, we all have to make a leap of faith, and the only real question is whether that leap is to be toward the stars or into Atkins' dunghill.

For me, the choice is clear. I believe the universe was created as a home for man and I therefore find Christ's admonition most appropriate. *"Be not afraid!"* is a watchword that we can adopt as our own because we are children of the universe, reflections of an Eternal Spirit, not orphans in a hostile world. The universe was created for us and our kind, and our journey, I am convinced, is forever.

EPILOGUE

"This life's five windows of the soul
Distorts the Heavens from pole to pole,
and leads you to believe a lie
When you see with, not thro', the eye."
        –*William Blake*

Shortly after I had penned the final words of my summary, I came across a new book by the eminent English physicist, John Polkinghorne, who is also an Anglican priest. Polkinghorne's book is entitled *The Faith of a Physicist*, and it prompted me to re-read an earlier work of his, *Science and Creation: The Search for Understanding.** I had already resolved to add a few thoughts to my concluding chapter, and the perusal of Polkinghorne's latest writings gave me an additional incentive to do so.

In his chapter on *Eschatology* Polkinghorne writes:

> "I do not think that the eventual futility of the universe, over a time-scale of tens of billions of years, is very different in the theological problems it poses, from the eventual futility of ourselves, over a time-scale of tens of years... What is at issue is the faithfulness of God, the everlasting seriousness with which he regards his creatures... Our belief in a destiny beyond death rests ultimately on our belief that God is faithful and that he will not allow anything of good to be lost... It is not sufficient...to think simply of a return of the many to the One, the re-absorption of the drops of our being in the ocean of divine Being. That would produce a 'blessedness in which

---

The Faith of a Physicist: Reflections of a Bottom-up Thinker, The Gifford Lectures for 1993-94, by John Polkinghorne, Princeton University Press, 1995

there would be no blessed'... Because human relationships are part of the good that we presently experience...one must rightly expect their restoration and fulfillment in the world to come..."

Expanding on this theme, Polkinghorne continues:

"My understanding of the soul is that it is the almost infinitely complex, dynamic, information-bearing pattern carried at any instant by the matter of my animated body and continuously developing throughout all the constituent changes of my bodily make-up during the course of my earthly life... If you take me apart you will find that all you get will be matter—in all the elusive subtlety that quantum mechanics has taught us to attribute to the material—matter ultimately found to be constituted of the quarks, gluons, and electrons which compose all the rest of the physical universe. Neither soul nor entelechy will be found as a separate part of the residue. Yet if you want to encounter *me* you will have to refrain from that act of decomposition and accept me in my complex and delicately organized totality... That psychosomatic unity is dissolved at death by the decay of my body, but I believe it is a perfectly coherent hope that the pattern which is me will be remembered by God and its instantiation will be recreated by him when he reconstitutes me in a new environment of his choosing... Thus death is a real end but not the final end, for only God himself is ultimate."*

The reader will be well aware of my own views, and I do not think it necessary to reiterate them here. To me it is fascinating that Polkinghorne, an elementary particle physicist and former professor of mathematical physics at Cambridge University, should

---

*Quoted from *Faith of a Physicist* and *Science and Creation*, by John Polkinghorne

be able to reconcile his intimate knowledge of physics with what some might consider a 180 degree opposite position, the basic tenets of Christian theology. Obviously, such a reconciliation is possible, for others have also done it, notably Stanley L. Jaki, an ordained priest and a physicist holding a distinguished professorship at Seton Hall University in South Orange, New Jersey.

Science and theology are really not all that far apart when one thinks back to Zeno's paradox of motion and to the discontinuities which are often encountered in theoretical physics. The dilemma is the same one described by Leibnitz in his principle of sufficient reason: *Ex nihilo, nihilo fit.* Nothing comes from nothing. If we are spiritually real, that reality, like the reality of time and motion, must be unending. The reality of self is the continuous reality of the line, not the hypothetical reality of an infinite series of dimensionless juxtaposed points. Physics has shown that there is no 'hard' material core to anything, and that in the sub-atomic realm reality's 'bottom line' is seen to be only a frenetic dance of energy among fluctuating fields of evanescent waves and particles. There is never total destruction, only continual creation and re-creation. Energy is always conserved. The atom never decays completely; there is always a half-life remaining. But if this is true of the material world, must it not also be true of the noetic world of the mind and spirit? Does anything in that world ever cease to exist so long as there is a mind to contemplate it?

The universe is never without an Observer. The inexhaustible beating heart of the universe—the vacuum—with its infinite zero-point energy continues to pulsate even when the cosmic entropy has reached 100% and there is seemingly no motion remaining. Then, suddenly, a 'fluctuation', and a universe is born. Surely, no less than this must also be true of our noetic universe, the necessary spiritual counterpart of the material, for a coin always has two sides. A cup, to be a cup, must have both an inside and an outside. A universe, to *be* a universe, must be both material and spiritual. It follows, as the night the day, that—if the universe is unending—then so, too, are we.

".....And there was *LIGHT!*"

211

CHAPTER NOTES

PROLOGUE, pp. ix-xii

1. Luther, Ref. 101

PERCEIVING REALITY [Chapter 1], pp. 3-12

2. Einstein, Podolsky, Rosen: "Can quantum-mechanical description of physical reality be considered complete?", Physical Review, Vol. 47, 1935

3. Schrödinger, Ref. 136

4. See Chapter 17, *Mind and Consciousness,* for a fuller discussion.

5. Feynman, Ref. 46

6. Capra, Ref. 17

7. Bohm, Ref. 12

A REVOLUTION IN PHYSICS [Chapter 2], pp. 13-18

8. Lord Kelvin, a/k/a William Thompson

WORLDS WITHIN WORLDS [Chapter 3], pp. 19-22

9. Capra, Ref. 17

10. Bohm, Ref. 10

11. Bohm, Ref. 9

12. Albert Einstein, quoted in M. Capek, *The Philosophical Impact of Contemporary Physics*

THE PARADOXES OF PHYSICS [Chapter 4], pp. 23-28

13. The value of h = 6.6 X 10^{-27} erg-seconds.

14. Letter to Robert W. Wood, 1931, quoted in Mehra and Rechenberg, *The Historical Development of Quantum Theory,* Springer Verlag, 1982.

THE QUANTUM CONNECTION [Chapter 5], pp. 29-34

15. Pais, Ref. 115

16. Gribben, Ref. 59

17. Pais, Ref. 115. "There is no quantum world. There is only an abstract quantum physical description. It is wrong to think that the task of physics is to find out how nature is. Physics concerns what we can say about nature."

18. In the process of radioactive decay the atom's nucleus disintegrates 'spontaneously', apparently without cause, although in any large aggregation of radioactive atoms the overall decay rate is statistically predictable. The paradox of discreteness is evidenced here in that radioactivity never quite disappears from a sample of such atoms. The radioactivity is continuously

halved over a predictable span of time, getting closer and closer to zero without ever reaching it. Einstein believed radioactivity and quantum 'jumping' to be related and throughout his life he sought a causal explanation. None, to this date, has been found.

THE UNCERTAINTY PRINCIPLE [Chapter 6], pp. 35-44

19. More precisely, $h/2\pi$

20. Bohm, Ref. 10

21. Jaki, Ref. 80

22. Heisenberg, Ref. 65

23. Capra, Ref. 65. The vacuum, as understood quantum mechanically, is not 'empty', but is simply the lowest energy state of a physical system. Owing to quantum uncertainty, "There is a certain necessary and irreducible 'quiveriness' involved, which is called vacuum fluctuation." [John Polkinghorne, Ref. 125] The vacuum has a certain "zero-point energy", even when devoid of all matter or radiation. This zero-point energy is present throughout all of space. Thus the zero-point energy of the vacuum "appears as a vast omnipresent ocean of infinite energy". [Wallace, Ref. 156]

24. Heisenberg, Ref. 65

WAVE MECHANICS AND QUANTUM MYSTERY [Chapter 7], pp. 45-54

25. Peat, Ref. 118. "Jung's scarab" refers to a beetle which mysteriously flew into the psychiatrist's window just as a patient was relating a dream involving such an insect.

26. Heisenberg, Ref. 65

27. Feynman, Ref. 46

28. Gribben, Ref. 59

29. Gribben, Ref. 59

30. Feynman, Ref. 46

31. Bohm, Ref. 9

SCHRÖDINGER'S CAT AND ALL THAT [Chapter 8], pp. 55-62

32. A wave packet is essentially a group of waves with slightly different wave lengths and phases that have been superimposed on one another, such that they interfere *constructively* inside a small region of space and *destructively* outside it, thus rapidly reducing the wave amplitudes to zero.

33. This is the equation that appears on the first-day postmark of the Austrian stamp commemorating Schrödinger's 100th anniversary.

34. Moore, Ref. 107. Bohr's reply: "But the rest of us are very thankful for it - that you have - and your wave mechanics in its mathematical clarity and simplicity is a gigantic progress over the previous form of quantum mechanics."

35. It was this feature of the Copenhagen Interpretation which sorely vexed both Schrödinger and Einstein. In quantum theory the specific event can-

not be predicted; we can predict only the *probability* that it may happen. Einstein characterized the strangeness of this situation by referring to the wave function as a *Gespensterfeld*, that is, a "ghost field".

36. Bohm and Hiley, Ref. 13

THE EPR PARADOX: IS REALITY NON-LOCAL? (Chapter 9], pp. 63-74

37. A light cone is a space-time concept. In three-dimensional space light emanating from a point in space spreads out as a sphere in all directions, but in four-dimensional space-time it forms a conical structure. Events which lie inside the light cone can be causally connected; events which lie outside it cannot.

38. EPR: Albert Einstein, Boris Podolsky, Nathan Rosen

39. Bohr, N. (1935) *Physical Review.* 48. 696.

40. Moore, Ref. 107

41. Herbert, Ref. 66

42. Henry Stapp, *Nuovo Cimento* 40 B, 191, (1977)

FOR WHOM THE BELL TOLLS: THE INEQUALITY THEOREM (Chapter 10) pp. 75-92

43. Kafatos, Ref. 89

44. Baggott, Ref. 3

45. Pais, Ref. 114

46. Pais, Ref. 115

47. A nanosecond is 0.000000001 seconds, or one-billionth of a second.

48. Bell, J.S. (1981) *Journal de Physique.* Colloque C2, Suppl. au numéro 3, tome 42

49. Gary Zukav writes in *The Dancing Wu Li Masters:* "Every sub-atomic particle has a fixed, definite, and known angular momentum, but *nothing is spinning!* If you don't understand, don't worry. Physicists don't understand these words, either. They just use them."

50. Zukav, Ref. 168

51. Kafatos and Nadeau, Ref. 89

52. Quoted in Zukav, Ref. 168

THE ASPECT EXPERIMENTS [Chapter 11], pp. 93-98

53. Baggott, Ref. 3

54. Gribben, Ref. 59

55. Quoted in Baggott, Ref. 3

SEEING THINGS WHOLE [Chapter 12], pp. 101-112

56. Bohm, Ref. 9

57. D. Bohm and B. Hiley, "On the intuitive Understanding of Non-locality as implied by Quantum Theory", *Foundations of Physics,* 1975, Vol. 5

58. Bohm, Ref. 12

59. *Quantum Implications,* Essays in Honour of David Bohm, ed. by B.J. Hiley and F. David Peat, Routledge and Kegan Paul, Ltd., London, 1987

60. Moore, Ref. 107

61. Baggott, Ref. 3

62. Quoted in *Quantum Implications,* op. cit.

63. Bohm, D.J. and Hiley, B.J. Ref. 13

64. Bohm, Ref. 10

65. Hiley, B.J. and Peat, David [eds.], Ref. 69

BOHM'S QUANTUM ONTOLOGY [Chapter 13], pp. 113-130

66. Bohm, D. J. and Hiley, B.J., Ref. 13

67. Bohm and Hiley, Ref. 13

68. Luther, Ref. 101

69. Bohm and Hiley, Ref. 13

70. Bohm and Hiley, Ref. 13

71. Peat, Ref. 119

72. Bohm and Hiley, Ref. 13

73. Baggott, Ref. 3

74. Bohm and Hiley, Ref. 13

75. Bohm and Hiley, Ref. 13

76. Bohm and Hiley, Ref. 13

77. Bohm and Hiley, Ref. 13

78. Bohm, Ref. 10

79. Bohm and Hiley, Ref. 13. Also Hiley, B.J. and Peat, F. David, Ref. 69

80. Bohm and Hiley, Ref. 13

THE IMPLICATE ORDER [Chapter 14], pp. 131-138

81. Letter to Ernst Strauss, quoted by Penrose in Ref. 46

82. Hiley and Peat, Ref. 69

83. Bohm, Ref. 12

84. Bohm, *ibid*

85. Bohm, *ibid*

86. Bohm, *ibid.* On p. 151 of Ref. 12 Bohm defines what he means by the term *holomovement:*

    "To generalize, so as to emphasize undivided wholeness, we shall say that what 'carries' an implicate order is *the holomovement,* which is an unbroken and undivided totality. In certain cases we can abstract particular aspects of the holomovement (e.g. light, electrons, sound, etc.) but more generally all forms of the holomovement merge and are inseparable. Thus, in its totality, the holomovement is not limited in any specifiable way at all. It is not required to conform to any particular order, or to be bounded by any particular measure. Thus, *the holomovement is undefinable and immeasurable.*"

87. Bohm, *ibid*

A REALITY BEYOND PHYSICS [Chapter 15], pp. 139-152

88. Weinberg, Ref. 158

89. From his *Philosophical Dream*

90. Weinberg, Ref. 158

91. Jaki, Ref. 80

92. Kafatos and Nadeau, Ref. 89

93. Penrose, Ref. 121

94. Baggott, Ref. 3

95. Hooper and Teresi, Ref. 72

96. Huxley, Ref. 74

97. Kafatos and Nadeau, Ref. 89

98. Schrödinger, Ref. 137

99. Jaki, Ref. 80

THE PERSONIFICATION OF SELF [Chapter 16], pp. 153-166

100. Cornwell, John [ed.], Ref. 22

101. Schrödinger, Ref. 136

102. Schrödinger, *ibid*

103. Schrödinger, Ref. 137

104. Schrödinger, Ref. 135

105. Gribbin, Ref. 60. In addition, mutations sometimes occur, thereby modifying the genome.

106. Cornwell, John [ed.], Ref. 22, quoted by Oliver Sacks

107. Gribben, Ref. 60

108. Tomlin, Ref. 153

109. *Dualism,* strictly speaking, is the view that the world consists of, or is explicable as, two fundamental entities, such as spirit and matter, and that there is a phenomenal distinction between the physical and mental processes. Monism, on the other hand, conceives of the world as a unified whole. What I am intent on emphasizing here is the unity of opposites which give meaning to the whole. Both perspectives are needed for completeness, and that is why Bohr's concept of *complementarity* seems so à propos.

Bohr's views on *complementarity,* referring to the way he saw the paradoxical wave/particle relationship, were first publicly expressed at the 1927

Como [Italy] conference honoring the centenary of Alessandro Volta's death. Unfortunately, he was never able to sharpen his concept of complementarity in a manner to satisfy Einstein. Bohr's friend and colleague, Léon Rosenfeld, once recalled that "Bohr felt that whenever you come up with a definite statement about anything, you are betraying complementarity ..." [Interview by T.S. Kuhn and J.L. Heilbron, 22 July, 1963]. Bohr's coat-of-arms, the Yin/Yang symbol, contained the motto: *Contraria Complementa Sunt.*

110. Schrödinger, Ref. 135

MIND AND CONSCIOUSNESS [Chapter 17], pp. 167-184

111. Beckwith, *Religion, Philosophy, and Science,* N.Y. Philosophical Library, 1957

112. B.F. Skinner, "Behaviorism at 50", in *Behaviorism and Phenomenology,* ed. T.W. Swann, University of Chicago Press, 1964

113. Dean Wooldridge, *The Machinery of the Brain,* McGraw-Hill, N.Y., 1963

114. Erdmann and Stover, Ref. 39

115. Erdmann and Stover, *ibid*

116. Erdmann and Stover, *ibid*

117. Hooper and Teresi, Ref. 72

118. Cornwell, John [ed.], Ref. 22

119. Cornwell, John [ed.], *ibid*

120. Penrose, Roger Ref. 121

121. Zohar, Danah Ref. 167

122. Kafatos and Nadeau, Ref. 89

123. Kafatos and Nadeau, *ibid*

124. Bohm, David, Ref. 12 [See also Chapter Note 86]

125. Bohm, *ibid*

126. Bohm, *ibid*

127. Bohm, *ibid*

128. Otto, Rudolph Ref. 113

129. Tomlin, E.W.F. Ref. 152

130. Tomlin, *ibid*

OF TIME AND ENTROPY [Chapter 18], pp. 185-196

131. Coveney and Highfield, Ref. 23

132. Black hole: A collapsed star which is so compact that not even light can escape its gravitational grip.

133. The concept of entropy relates to the Second Law of Thermodynamics. The First Law of Thermodynamics, in contrast, establishes the conservation of energy in a physical process, though the form of that energy may vary.

134. Quoted in Barrow and Tipler, Ref. 6

135. Coveney and Highfield, Ref. 23

136. Penrose, Ref. 121

137. Penrose, *ibid*

A SUMMING-UP [Chapter 19], pp. 197-208

138. Penrose, Ref. 121

139. Newton's Third Law: To every action there is an equal and opposite reaction.

140. Albert Einstein, *Ideas and Opinions*, Crown Publishers, New York, 1954

141. Jaki, Ref. 80

142. C.S. Lewis, *The Personal Heresy in Criticism*, Essays and Studies by Members of the English Association, (1933-34), p. 28

143. Baggott, Ref. 3

144. Baggott, *ibid*

145. Einstein, *op. cit.*

146. Quoted in Baggott, Ref. 3

APPENDIX A

BELL'S THEOREM AND
THE POLARIZATION EXPERIMENT

The polarization experiment can be confusing owing to the many unfamiliar concepts and terms with which it is concerned.

Basically, what we are dealing with in the polarization experiment are pairs of polarized photons that have been emitted from a common source with zero angular momentum and are then allowed to travel away from one another in opposite directions. Photons emitted in this way are said to be in the twin state; when measured along a common axis they are always identical to one another. Either photon by itself may be "up" or "down", i.e. "vertical" or "horizontal" whenever it is measured, as the two possible directions of a photon's polarization are called. But, so long as both photons' polarizations are measured along a common axis, it is mathematically certain that one photon's polarization will always be found to be the same as the other's. What we are interested in finding out is how the correlation between photon "A" and photon"B" changes as we measure their polarizations along *different* axes.

To do this we use calcite crystals placed at either end of the route of travel of the two photons. Imagine each calcite crystal as having the face of a clock which encircles the axis of travel at either end. [See Fig. 4] The axis of travel may be visualized as the axel of an automobile where the wheels at both ends correspond to the clock faces of the measuring instruments, the two calcite crystals. The emission source of the paired photons is then situated at the midpoint of the automobile axel. We can visualize, initially, two possible situations:

Situation One

In this situation the optical axes of *both* calcite crystals (the polarization analyzers or filters) are parallel, i.e. vertically aligned with one another, as would be the case if both axes (filters) were pointing to 12 o ' clock . We designate this vertical alignment of both optical axes of the crystals as constituting an angle of *zero degrees* between them. When the axes of the crystals, the polarization analyzers, are thus aligned, there is 100% correlation between the polarizations of both photons. That is, when the calcite crystal finds the photon passing through it to be polarized in the twelve o' clock direction, it is 100% certain that its twin, passing through the second crystal, will be identically polarized; and if it finds the photon passing through it to be polarized in an orthogonal direction, that is, at right angles to its own optical axis, it is 100% certain that the other photon, passing through the second analyzer, will also be orthogonally polarized. *Note that each photon, by itself, may be polarized in either direction,* but that this direction is *either* always vertical (along the optical axis) or always horizontal (at 90 degrees to the optical axis). Whether vertical or horizontal, the polarizations are always identical for both photons. This is what is *meant* by 100% positive correlation. It occurs *only* when the optical axes of both crystals

FIGURE 4

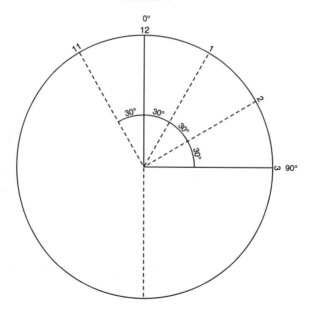

are aligned in the same plane, and it is normally designated by a value of +1.

Situation Two

In situation two we *rotate* one of the crystals by 90 degrees so that its optical axis is now horizontal rather than vertical. This means, in terms of the clock face, that one optical axis will now be pointing to three o'clock while the other will be pointing to twelve o'clock. The joint angle between the two optical axes is now 90 degrees, whereas in situation one it was zero degrees. The polarizations of the paired photons are now completely reversed. There is now 100% negative, or anti, correlation between the two photons. Perfect anti-correlation of the two photons is normally assigned a value of -1.

There is no disagreement between quantum and classical theory as to this result. Where they disagree profoundly is what happens in the next two situations:

Situation Three

Suppose we leave the optical axis of the first crystal at 12 o'clock but rotate the axis of the second crystal to 1 o'clock. The relative angle between the two crystals will now be 30 degrees. At this angle we find that the polarizations are no longer 100% positively matched, but neither are they 100% negatively mis-matched. Rather, a fraction of them are mis-matched, and this fraction can be accurately calculated by quantum theory. At an angle of 30 degrees quantum theory predicts that there will be one mis-match out of every four, because $\cos^2 30 = .75$. The value of .75, or 3/4, gives the proportion of *matches* in a series of polarization measurements, so that .25, or 1/4, equals the proportion of mis-matches. *This proportion is the same whether we rotate filter "A", the first calcite crystal, by 30 degrees off parallel or whether we rotate filter "B" by the same amount, in either direction.* The only thing that matters is the relative angle between the optical axes of the two crystals.

Situation Three

Now, here is the interesting part. I am going to give it to you in the words of Nick Herbert, author of *Quantum Reality: Beyond the New Physics* [Ref. 66] because he so delightfully dramatizes the action. He assumes the calcites in the experiment are separated by a distance of 500 light-years, the first being located on Earth and the second on the star Betelgeuse, where two "operators" are variously turning their crystals.
Nick Herbert:

"Now we are ready to demonstrate Bell's proof. Watch closely; this proof is so short that it goes by fast. Align the calcites at 12 o'clock. Observe that the messages [correlations] are identical. Move [calcite "A"] by 30 degrees. Note that the messages are no longer the same but contain "errors"—one miss out of every four marks. Move [calcite "A"] back to twelve and these errors disappear; the messages are the same again. Whenever "A" is moved by 30 degrees in either direction, we see the messages differ by one character out of four. Moving "A" back to twelve o'clock restores the identity of the two messages. The same thing happens on Betelgeuse. With both calcites set at twelve noon, messages are identical. When [the Betelgeuse operator] moves [calcite "B"] by 30 degrees in either direction, we see the messages differ by one part in four. Moving "B" calcite back to twelve noon restores the identity of the two messages."

But now see what happens. When we turn calcite "A", by 30 degrees in one direction and then turn calcite "B" by 30 degrees in the other direction, we do not get the sum of the two effects. We get *three* mismatches out of four rather than the two we naively expect. At an angle of 60 degrees between the two calcites we get a totally unexpected result. Nick Herbert again:

"We assume that turning calcite "A" can change only the "A" message; likewise, turning calcite "B" can change only the "B" message. This is Bell's famous locality assumption. It is identical to the assumption Einstein made in his EPR paradox: that (one) observer's acts cannot affect (another) observer's results. The locality assumption—that "A"'s acts don't change "B"'s code—seems entirely reasonable: how could an action on Betelgeuse change what's happening right now on Earth?"

According to local reality theory, it can't. If the two calcite crystals moved separately give a certain result, the fact that they are *both* moved should produce the sum of the two results—assuming, of course, that they are truly independent. It was on that assumption, the assumption of independence, said Einstein, that "we should absolutely hold fast: the real factual situation of the system "A" is independent of what is done with the system "B" which is spatially separated from it." [Ref. 66]

This, however, is not the case. The Aspect experiments conclusively validated the predictions of quantum theory that the two quantum systems are inter-related, notwithstanding the fact that they may possess "Einstein separability" and may be millions of miles apart from one another in space. Hence, the locality assumption must be false. There must be non-local influences at work to produce so curious a result. The polarizations of the two photons in the EPR experiment are correlated much more strongly than any local reality theory can explain.

APPENDIX B

A NOTE ON COMPLEMENTARITY
AND NON-LOCALITY

In their enormously insightful book *The Conscious Universe* [Ref. 89] Menas Kafatos and Robert Nadeau describe three types of non-locality—the spatial, the temporal, and a third type which is essentially a unification of the other two. Type I, spatial non-locality, is what is implied by quantum theory as verified by the Aspect experiments. Type II, temporal non-locality, is what seems to be implied by certain "delayed choice" experiments in which observation of the event appears able to influence what actually happened *in the past*. Type III non-locality refers to the unified whole that is expressed by the entire physical space-time situation.

Kafatos and Nadeau argue that type II non-locality, i.e. *temporal non-locality*, "must also now be viewed as a fact of nature", along with spatial non-locality, because both are *complementary aspects* of a single unified reality in which there are non-local connections between certain quantum events not only in terms of distance but also in terms of time. Temporal non-locality implies that these spatially non-local events are also insensitive to the arrow of time. This proposition, in my view, is even more mind-boggling, if that is possible, than the superluminal connections that have been shown to exist under type I non-locality.

These two types of non-locality, the spatial and the temporal, are complementary aspects of an *undivided wholeness* in the cosmos. Together, they represent a sort of 'event horizon' "beyond which science cannot venture". "The ultimate character of this wholeness... (lies)...completely outside the domain of scientific knowledge... Science, in our new situation, cannot say anything about reality-in-itself, because the existence of the whole can never be disclosed by mathematical physics. The simple and straightforward explanation of why this is the case is that both aspects of the manner in which this whole manifests in physical reality [i.e. the spatial and the temporal] cannot, in accordance with the logical principle of complementarity, be 'simultaneously' disclosed."

"Herein lies the paradox: Scientific knowledge conditions us into an awareness of this whole and yet cannot fully affirm or 'prove' its existence in scientific terms... The best religious thinkers have (generally) been inclined to accept this limitation, (but)... the community of physicists, in general, has not. We are personally in agreement with Capra who has rather consistently argued for a belief in ontology, or in the existence of a Being that is not and cannot be the sum of beings .. and we are very much in agreement with Bohm's conclusion that undivided wholeness implies that no categorical distinction can be made between the dynamics of human consciousness and those of the entire cosmos... Science in our new situation in no way argues against the existence of God or Being...(yet) the mystery that evades all human understanding remains. The study of physical reality should only take us perpetually closer to that horizon of knowledge...while never being able to comprehend or explain this mystery."

Kafatos and Nadeau conclude with this thought: "...One clearly does not arrive at a belief in an ontology...based on the 'practical' necessity of doing so... In our view the majority of human beings do apprehend or intuit on the deepest levels of their subjective experience the existence of Being as a self-evident truth... Such a belief requires, as Kierkegaard pointed out, a 'leap of faith' that may have little or nothing to do with the dictates of reason."

APPENDIX C

A NOTE ON REALITY

The paradox of what is real is perhaps the oldest one in philosophy. To the man in the street it is a dumb question, because he is faced with the reality of survival every day. To Einstein it was also a 'dumb' question (although Einstein was not deceived), because he was a realist who was unshakeably convinced that there was a material universe "out there" which ran independently, so-to-speak, of man's perceptions. Yet Einstein's own theory of relativity embodied a measure of observer-dependence; The sequence of events in space-time—and hence their 'reality'—was not the same for everyone. Neils Bohr took observer-dependence to an extreme; nothing was real in his quantum world until it had been observed, and then only as a series of pointer readings. What was *really* going on in the sub-atomic realm, he maintained, was meaningless and unknowable.

Physicists have become troubled by this question only recently, but philosophers from Plato to Berkeley have debated it for centuries. It is not a trivial question, and it lay at the heart of the entire EPR debate. The discovery of non-local causes notwithstanding, the greatest physicists of the century have not been able to solve it. The mystery has simply retreated still further over the horizon.

My own view of the matter is more Berkeleyan than realist. I believe that *esse est percipi*—to be is to be perceived—but I also believe that more than mind is involved. The relation between perception and reality is complementary, or dualistic, because perception necessitates *both* subject and object; the artist's creation requires a canvas and paints.

The material world is the backdrop for our reality, but perception is what we make of it. There is literally an infinity of unique perceptions depending on the perceiver and the scale of observation. There is no single "one size fits all" description of reality. When we speak of an independent reality beyond the perceived, a universe that is "ticking away" regardless of whether we are looking at it or not, it is almost impossible to state precisely what we mean. Laws and principles exist, or we would have a chaos, but beyond that all is flux and change. The atom itself is mostly empty space.

As both participants in, and observers of, the universe we have to admire the cleverness of this arrangement, we have to stand in awe of it. It is one in which a Supreme Intelligence, a Supreme Artist, is continually creating and in which we, his creation, are free to perceive ourselves in the canvas and perhaps even to modify it within the limits of our abilities. As Jim Baggott has noted, "Whatever the nature of reality, it cannot be as simple as we might have thought ..."* A measure of faith is required to accept it, but—like Margaret Fuller—we have little choice in the matter. In the last analysis, reality turns out to be both objective and subjective—in other words, it is complementary. We live in a dualistic reality that is at least in part what we make of it.

---

*The Meaning of Quantum Theory (Ref. 2), p. 148

SOURCES AND REFERENCES

1. ASIMOV, Isaac, *The Collapsing Universe*, Pocket Books, New York, 1978

2. ATTENBOROUGH, David, *Life on Earth*, Little, Brown & Co., Boston, Toronto, 1979

3. BAGGOTT, Jim, *The Meaning of Quantum Theory*, Oxford University Press, New York, 1992

4. BARROW, John D., *Theories of Everything*, The Quest for Ultimate Explanation, Ballantine Books, New York, 1991

5. BARROW, John D., *The World within the World*, Clarendon Press, Oxford, 1988

6. BARROW, John D. and TIPLER, Frank J., *The Anthropic Cosmological Principle*, Oxford University Press, New York, 1988

7. BELL, J.S., *Speakable and Unspeakable in Quantum Mechanics*, Cambridge University Press, Cambridge, 1987

8. BEROFSKY, B., [ed.] *Free Will and Determinism*, Harper & Row, New York, 1966

9. BOHM, David, *Quantum Theory*, Prentice-Hall, New York, 1951

10. BOHM, David, *Causality and Chance in Modern Physics*, Harper & Bros., New York, 1957

11. BOHM, D.J. and HILEY, B.J., *On the Intuitive Understanding of Non-Locality as Implied by Quantum Theory*, Foundations of Physics, Vol. 5, No. 1, Plenum Publishing Corp., 1975

12. BOHM, David, *Wholeness and the Implicate Order*, Routledge, London, 1980

13. BOHM, D.J. and HILEY, B.J., *The Undivided Universe*, An Ontological Interpretation of Quantum Theory, Routledge, London, 1993

14. BRONOWSKI, J., *Science and Human Values*, Harper & Row, New York, 1956

15. BRONOWSKI, J., *The Ascent of Man*, Little, Brown & Co., Boston, 1973

16. CALDER, Nigel, *Einstein's Universe*, Viking Penguin, New York, 1979

17. CAPRA, Fritjof, *The Tao of Physics*, New Science Library, Shambhala, Boston, 1985

18. CARROLL, Lewis, *Alice in Wonderland and Through the Looking Glass*, Grosset & Dunlap, Inc., 1946

19. CASTI, John L., *Paradigms Lost*, Tackling the Unanswered Mysteries of Modern Science, Avon Books, New York, 1989

20. CHAISSON, Eric, *Relatively Speaking,* Relativity, Black Holes, and the Fate of the Universe, W.W. Norton & Co., New York, 1990

21. CHESTERTON, G.K., *The Everlasting Man,* Hoder & Stoughton, London, 1953

22. CORNWELL, John, [ed.], *Nature's Imagination,* The Frontiers of Scientific Vision, Oxford University Press, New York, Oxford, Melbourne, 1995

23. COVENEY, Peter and HIGHFIELD, Roger, *The Arrow of Time,* Fawcett Columbine, New York, 1990

24. CRICK, Francis, *Life Itself: Its Origin and Nature,* Simon & Schuster, New York, 1982

25. DARLING, David, *Deep Time,* Dell Publishing, New York, 1989

26. DARWIN, Charles, *The Origin of Species* (1859) and *The Descent of Man,* (1871), Random House, Modern Library, New York

27. DAVIES, Paul, *The Runaway Universe,* Harper & Row, New York, 1978

28. DAVIES, Paul, *The Edge of Infinity,* Simon & Schuster, New York, 1981

29. DAVIES, Paul, *God and the New Physics,* Simon & Schuster, New York, 1983

30. DAVIES, Paul, *The Mind of God,* Simon & Schuster, New York, 1992

31. DAVIES, Paul and GRIBBEN, John, *The Matter Myth,* Simon & Schuster, New York, 1992

32. DAWKINS, Richard, *The Selfish Gene,* Oxford University Press, New York, 1976

33. D'ESPAGNAT, Bernard, *Reality and the Physicist,* Knowledge, Duration, and the Quantum World, Cambridge University Press, Cambridge, 1989

34. DUNN, L.C. and DOBZHANSKY, Th., *Heredity, Race, and Society,* New American Library, New York, 1952

35. DU NOÜY, Lecompte, *Human Destiny,* New American Library, New York, 1949

36. DYSON, Freeman, *Infinite in all Directions,* Harper & Row, New York, 1988

37. DYSON, Freeman, *From Eros to Gaia,* Pantheon Books, New York, 1992

38. EDDINGTON, Sir Arthur, *The Expanding Universe,* Ann Arbor Paperbacks, University of Michigan, Ann Arbor, 1958

39. ERDMANN, Erika and STOVER, David, *Beyond a World Divided:* Human Values in the Brain-Mind Science of Roger Sperry, Shambhala, Boston, 1991

40. EINSTEIN, Albert, *The Principle of Relativity,* Methuen & Co., Ltd., London, 1923

41. EINSTEIN, Albert, *The World As I See It,* Citadel Press, New York, 1979

42. EISELY, Loren, *The Immense Journey,* Vintage Books, New York, 1959

43. EISELY, Loren, *The Unexpected Universe*, Harcourt, Brace and World, New York, 1969

44. EISELY, LOREN, *All the Strange Hours*, Charles Scribner's Sons, New York, 1975

45. FEYNMAN, Richard, *Q.E.D.—The Strange Theory of Light and Matter*, Princeton University Press, Princeton, N.J., 1985

46. FEYNMAN, Richard, *The Character of Physical Law*, M.I.T. Press, Cambridge, Mass. 1990

47. FINE, Arthur, *The Shaky Game:* Einstein Realism and the Quantum Theory, University of Chicago Press, 1986

48. FLEW, Anthony, *Body, Mind, and Death*, The Macmillan Company, New York, 1964

49. FLOOD, Raymond and LOCKWOOD, Michael, [eds.], *The Nature of Time*, Basil Blackwell, Ltd., Oxford, 1986

50. FRANK, Philipp, *Foundations of Physics*, Vol. 1 No. 7 of International Encyclopedia of Unified Science, University of Chicago Press, Chicago, 1946

51. GAMOW, George, *One, Two, Three...Infinity*, New American Library, New York, 1953

52. GAMOW, George, *Mr. Tompkins in Paperback*, Cambridge University Press, London, 1957

53. GAMOW, George, *Biography of the Earth*, New American Library, New York, 1958

54. GAMOW, George, *Thirty Years that Shook Physics*, The Story of Quantum Theory, Doubleday, New York, 1966

55. GARDNER, Martin [ed.], *Great Essays in Science*, Pocket Books, New York, 1957

56. GARDNER, Martin, *The Relativity Explosion*, Vintage Books, New York, 1976

57. GLEICK, James, *Genius*, The Life and Science of Richard Feynman, Pantheon Books, New York, 1992

58. GOULD, Stephen Jay, *Ever Since Darwin*, W.W. Norton & Co., New York, 1979

59. GRIBBIN, John, *In Search of Schrödinger's Cat*, Quantum Physics and Reality, Bantam Books, New York, 1984

60. GRIBBIN, John, *In Search of the Double Helix*, Quantum Physics and Life, Bantam Books, New York, 1987

61. GRIFFIN, Donald R., *The Question of Animal Awareness*, The Rockefeller University Press, New York, 1981

62. HAWKING, Stephen W., *A Brief History of Time*, Bantam Books, New York, 1988

63. HAYWARD, Jeremy W., *Perceiving Ordinary Magic:* Science and Intuitive Wisdom, New Science Library, Shambhala, Boston, 1984

64. HAYWARD, Jeremy, *Shifting Worlds, Changing Minds,* Where the Sciences and Buddhism Meet, New Science Library, Shambhala, Boston, 1987

65. HEISENBERG, Werner, *Physics and Philosophy,* Harper and Row, New York, 1958

66. HERBERT, Nick, *Quantum Reality:* Beyond the New Physics, Anchor/Doubleday, New York, 1985

67. HERBERT, Nick, *Elemental Mind:* Human Consciousness and the New Physics, Penguin Books, New York, 1993

68. HIGHET, Gilbert, *Man's Unconquerable Mind,* Columbia University Press, New York, 1954

69. HILEY, B.J. and PEAT, F. David, [eds.] *Quantum Implications:* Essays in Honour of David Bohm, Routledge and Kegan Paul, London, 1987

70. HOFSTADTER, Douglas R., *Gödel, Escher, Bach: An Eternal Golden Braid,* Random House, New York, 1979

71. HOFSTADTER, Douglas R. and DENNETT, Daniel C., *The Mind's I—Fantasies and Reflections on Self and Soul,* Basic Books, New York, 1981

72. HOOPER, Judith and TERESI, Dick, *The Three Pound Universe, the Brain,* Dell Publishing, New York, 1986

73. HOYLE, Fred, *The Nature of the Universe,* New American Library, New York, 1955

74. HUXLEY, Aldous, *The Perennial Philosophy,* Chato and Windus, Ltd., London, 1954

75. HUXLEY, Julian, *Evolution in Action,* New American Library, New York, 1953

76. HUXLEY, Julian, *Man in the Modern World,* New American Library, New York, 1953

77. HUXLEY, Julian, *Religion Without Revelation,* Max Parrish & Co., Ltd., London, 1957

78. IRVINE, William, *Apes, Angels, and Victorians,* Weidenfeld and Nicolson, London, 1955

79. JACKSON, Francis and MOORE, Patrick, *Life in the Universe,* W.W. Norton & Co., New York, 1987

80. JAKI, Stanley L., *God and the Cosmologists,* Regnery Gateway, Washington, D.C., 1989

81. JAMES, William, *The Varieties of Religious Experience,* The Gifford Lectures for 1901-02, Longmans, Green and Co., London

82. JAMES, William, *The Will to Believe,* and Other Essays, Longmans, Green and Co., London

83. JEANS, Sir James, *Physics and Philosophy*, Dover Publications, New York, 1981 [originally published by Cambridge University Press, 1943]

84. JEANS, Sir James, *The Mysterious Universe*, Cambridge University Press, Cambridge, 1948

85. JOHNSON, Phillip E., *Darwin on Trial*, Regnery Gateway, Washington, D.C., 1991

86. POPE JOHN PAUL II, *Crossing the Threshold of Hope*, Alfred A. Knopf, New York, 1994

87. JUDSON, Horace, *The Eighth Day of Creation*, Simon & Schuster, New York, 1982

88. KAFATOS, Menas [ed.], *Bell's Theorem, Quantum Theory, and Conceptions of the Universe*, Kluwer Academic Publishers, Heidelberg, 1989

89. KAFATOS, Menas and NADEAU, Robert, *The Conscious Universe*, Part and Whole in Modern Physical Theory, Springer Verlag, Heidelberg, 1990

90. KÖSTLER, Arthur, *The Roots of Coincidence*, Random House, New York, 1973

91. KRISHNAMURTI, J. and BOHM, David, *The Ending of Time*, Krishnamurti Foundation Trust, Ltd., HarperSanFrancisco, 1985

92. KUHN, Thomas S., *The Structure of Scientific Revolutions*, Vol. 2, No 2 of International Encyclopedia of Unified Science, University of Chicago Press, Chicago, 1962

93. KÜNG, Hans, *Does God Exist?*, An Answer for Today, Doubleday, New York, 1980

94. LACHS, John, *Mind and Philosophers*, Vanderbilt University Press, Nashville, Tenn., 1987

95. LASZLO, Ervin, *Evolution: The Grand Synthesis*, New Science Library, Shambhala, Boston, 1987

96. LAYZER, David, *Cosmogenesis: The Growth of Order in the Universe*, Oxford University Press, New York, 1990

97. LESHAN, Lawrence and MARGENAU, Henry, *Einstein's Space and Van Gogh's Sky*, Macmillan, New York, 1982

98. LEWIS, C.S., *Miracles*, Geoffrey Bles, London, 1952

99. LEWIS, C.S., *The Problem of Pain*, Geoffrey Bles, London, 1952

100. LIGHTMAN, Alan and BRAWER, Roberta, *Origins: The Lives and Worlds of Modern Cosmologists*, Harvard University Press, Cambridge, Mass., 1990

101. LUTHER, Martin E.W., *The Compasses of God*, Science and Human Destiny, Marwolf Publishing, Minneapolis, Minnesota, 1991

102. LUTHER, Steven W., *Bio-Cultural Evolution*, [unpublished MS], Minneapolis, Minn., 1977

103. MALINOWSKI, Bronislaw, *Magic, Science, and Religion*, Doubleday, New York, 1948

104. McCANN, Lester, *Blowing the Whistle on Darwinism*, Graphic Publishing Co., Lake Mills, IA, 1986

105. MEDAWAR, Peter, *The Limits of Science*, Oxford University Press, New York, 1984

106. MOORE, Ruth, *The Coil of Life*, Alfred A. Knopf, New York, 1961

107. MOORE, Walter, *Schrödinger, Life and Thought*, Cambridge University Press, Cambridge, 1989

108. MORRIS, Richard, *The Edges of Science: Crossing the Boundary from Physics to Metaphysics*, Prentice Hall Press, New York, 1990

109. OPARIN, A.I., *The Chemical Origin of Life*, Charles C. Thomas, Springfield IL, 1964

110. ORGEL, Leslie, *The Origins of Life*, John Wiley & Sons, New York, 1973

111. ORGEL, Leslie and MILLER, Stanley, *The Origins of Life on Earth*, Prentice Hall, New York, 1974

112. ORNSTEIN, Robert and SOBEL, David, *The Healing Brain*, Simon & Schuster, New York, 1987

113. OTTO, Rudolph, *The Idea of the Holy*, Oxford University Press, London, 1950

114. PAIS, Abraham, *Subtle is the Lord: The Science and the Life of Albert Einstein*, Oxford University Press, Oxford, 1982

115. PAIS, Abraham, *Neils Bohr's Times*, in Physics, Philosophy, and Polity, Clarendon Press, Oxford, 1991

116. PARK, David, *The Image of Eternity: Roots of Time in the Physical World*, University of Massachusetts Press, Amherst, 1980

117. PEAT, F. David, *Superstrings and the Search for a Theory of Everything*, Contemporary Books, Chicago, 1988

118. PEAT, F. David, *Synchronicity: The Bridge Between Matter and Mind*, Bantam Books, New York, 1987

119. PEAT, F. David, *Einstein's Moon*, Bell's Theorem and the Curious Quest for Quantum Reality, Contemporary Books, Chicago, 1990

120. PEIRCE, Charles S., *Values in a Universe of Chance*, Doubleday, New York, 1958

121. PENROSE, Roger, *The Emperor's New Mind*, Oxford University Press, Oxford, 1989

122. PENROSE, Roger, *Shadows of the Mind*, Oxford University Press, 1994

123. POLKINGHORNE, J.C., *The Quantum World*, Princeton University Press, Princeton, 1989

124. POLKINGHORNE, J.C., *Science and Creation*, New Science Library, Shambhala, Boston, 1989

125. POLKINGHORNE, John, *The Faith of a Physicist*, The Gifford Lectures for 1993-4, Princeton University Press, Princeton, 1994

126. POUNDSTONE, William, *Labyrinths of Reason*, Doubleday, New York, 1988

127. PONOMOREV, L.I., *The Quantum Dice*, Institute of Physics Publishing, Bristol, 1993

128. PRIGOGINE, Ilya and STENGERS, Isabelle, *Order out of Chaos*, New Science Library, Shambhala, Boston, 1984

129. REIDY, David and WALLACE, Ken, *The Solar System: A Practical Guide*, Allen and Unwin, Sydney, 1991

130. RESTAK, Richard, *The Mind*, Bantam Books, New York, 1983

131. RUSSELL, Bertrand, *Religion and Science*, Oxford Universty Press, Oxford, 1956

132. RUSSELL, Bertrand, *The Problems of Philosophy*, Galaxy, Oxford, 1959

133. RUSSELL, Bertrand, *The ABC of Relativity*, New American Library, New York, 1958

134. SAGAN, Carl, *The Dragons of Eden*, Ballantine Books, New York, 1977

135. SCHRÖDINGER, Erwin, *What is Life?*, Doubleday, New York, 1956

136. SCHRÖDINGER, Erwin, *Mind and Matter*, The Tarner Lectures, Trinity College, Cambridge, 1956

137. SCHRÖDINGER, Erwin, *My View of the World*, Cambridge University Press, Cambridge, 1964

138. SCHWEITZER, Albert, *Life and Message*, Beacon Press, Boston, 1950

139. SCHWEITZER, Albert, *Out of My Life and Thought*, New American Library, New York, 1953 [reprint]

140. SCOTT, Andrew, *The Creation of Life*—Past, Future, Alien, Basil Blackwell, Ltd., Oxford, 1986

141. SCOTT, Andrew [ed.], *The Frontiers of Science*, Basil Blackwell, Ltd., Oxford, 1992

142. SEARLE, John, *The Rediscovery of the Mind*, M.I.T. Press, Cambridge, Mass., 1992

143. SILK, Joseph, *The Big Bang*, W.H. Freeman & Co., New York, 1989

144. SIMPSON, George Gaylord, *The Meaning of Evolution*, New American Library, New York, 1955

145. SKLAR, Lawrence, *Space, Time, and Spacetime*, University of California Press, Berkeley and Los Angeles, 1956

146. SNOW, C.P., *The Physicists*, Little, Brown & Co., Boston, 1981

147. SULLIVAN, J.W.N., *The Limitations of Science*, New American Library, New York, 1954

148. SWAMI PRABHAVANANDA and ISHERWOOD, Christopher, *The Song of God: Bhagavad-Gita*, New American Library, New York, 1969

149. TATE, G.W., *Origins*, Baxter, Ltd., London, 1949

150. TAYLOR, Gordon Rattray, *The Great Evolution Mystery*, Harper & Row, New York, 1983

151. THAXTON, Charles B., BRADLEY, Walter L., and OLSEN, Roger L., *The Mystery of Life's Origin: Re-assessing Current Theories*, The Philosophical Library, New York, 1984

152. TOMLIN, E.W.F., *The Approach to Metaphysics*, Kegan Paul, London, 1947

153. TOMLIN, E.W.F., *Great Philosophers of the Eastern World* and *Great Philosophers of the Western World*, A.A. Wyn, Inc., New York, 1952

154. TREFIL, James, *The Moment of Creation*, Macmillan, New York, 1983

155. VELIKOVSKY, I., *Worlds in Collision*, Delta, New York, 1965

156. WALLACE, B. Allan, *Choosing Reality*, New Science Library, Shambhala, Boston, 1989

157. WEINBERG, Steven, *The First Three Minutes*, Basic Books, New York, 1988

158. WEINBERG, Steven, *Dreams of a Final Theory*, Pantheon Books, New York, 1993

159. WEINER, Jonathan, *Planet Earth*, Bantam Books, New York, 1986

160. WELLS, H.G., *The Outline of History*, Doubleday, New York, 1956

161. WHITEHEAD, Alfred North, *Adventures of Ideas*, New American Library, New York, 1955

162. WHITEHEAD, Alfred North, *Science and Philosophy*, The Philosophical Library, New York, 1958

163. WILBER, Ken, *Quantum Questions*, New Science Library, Shambhala, Boston, 1985

164. WILL, Clifford M., *Was Einstein Right?*, Basic Books, New York, 1986

165. WORTH, C. and ENDERS, Robert K., *The Nature of Living Things*, New American Library, New York, 1955

166. WOLF, Fred Alan, *Taking the Quantum Leap*, Harper & Row, New York, 1981

167. ZOHAR, Danah, *The Quantum Self*, William Morrow and Co., New York, 1990

168. ZUKAV, Gary, *The Dancing Wu Li Masters*, Bantam Books, New York, 1980.

SUBJECT INDEX

NAME INDEX

ALLEN, Woody: 153, 202-203

ANDERSON, Poul: 146

ASPECT, Alain: The Aspect Experiments, Chapter 11; mentioned, x-xi, 73-76, 80-81, 90-91, 111-112, 122-123

ATKINS, Peter: 154, 159-160, 180-181, 207

BAGGOTT, Jim: 76-77, 93; Aspect Experiments, 94-95; pilot wave theory, 108-109; Popper's pinboard, 117-118; wave function, 122; reality, 143-144; mentioned, 199-200; on God, 204-206

BELL, John Stewart: The Inequality Theorem (see Chapter 10); x-xi, 44, 67-68, 73, 197

BLOCH, Arthur: Quoted, 185

BOHM, David: Overview, 10; infinity, 16, 140; uncertainty, 39-40; Copenhagen Interpretation, 52-53; wave function collapse, 60-61; Many Worlds, 71-72; quantum realism, 91-92; history, 101-102; quantum theory and wholeness, 102-103, 178-179; Schrödinger equation reformulated, 105-106, 108-109; reality, 106-107, 178-179; critics, 107-111; Quantum Potential, 110-114; ontology, Chapter 13; Implicate Order, Chapter 14, also 176-179; Ground, 146-147; radio analogy, 178; holomovement, 178; consciousness, 178-179

BOHR, Neils: and Einstein, 4, 81-82, 139; quantum reality, 4-5, 41, 47-48, 61, 65-66, 70-71, 76-77, 92, 122, 128-129; complementarity, 24-25, 47-48, 72-73, 146; history, 24-32; non-locality, 5, 33, 70, 81-82; wholeness, 64-65, 70, 90, 101-102, 127-128; EPR, 53, 62, 67-68, 77-78, 80, 90-91; atomic theory, 31-32; quantum jumps, 31-33, 110-111; classical physics, 33; Heisenberg, 40; Schrödinger, 57-58; wave 'packet', 58; indeterminacy, 65-66; observables, 127-128; Copenhagen Interpretation, 59-60; measurement, 122; God, 139; Quantum Potential, 110-111; quoted, 29, 76-77; other mention, 57-60, 78-80, 84-85, 90, 92, 101-102, 107-108

BORN, Max: On Schrödinger Equation, 46-47, 49-50, 56-57

CAPRA, Fritjof: Wholeness, 10, 15-16; energy, 21-22; particles and fields, 22; vacuum, 41-42

CARLYLE, Thomas: Quoted, 3, 200

CARROLL, Lewis: Quoted, 55

CLAUSER, John: 93

CLAUSIUS, Rudolph: Entropy, 190

COVENEY, Peter, and *HIGHFIELD,* Roger: 186

D'ALIBARD, Jean: 93

Books by Martin E.W. Luther are directly available
by calling or writing:

Marwolf Publishing
6941 Morgan Avenue South
Minneapolis, Minnesota 55423
(612) 869-4579
or
(800) 484-2273
Ext. 1466